Enlightenment Dialogues

A Journey of Post-metaphysical Onliness Awakening

by

Martin Treon

2

Auroral Skies Press
13348 S. 176th Lane
Goodyear, Arizona 85338
2011

Copyright 2011 by Martin Treon
Cover design by Martin Treon
See Facebook: Martin Treon
See Facebook: Auroral Skies Press

Library of Congress Control Number: 2011905361
ISBN: Soft cover   978-1-4628-8988-4
                     Ebook   978-1-4628-8989-1

1. Consciousness 2. I Ching   3. Enlightenment.

Book manufacture, production and distribution by Xlibris Corporation,
    International Plaza II, Suite 410, Philadelphia, PA 19113.

All rights reserved. No part of this book may be reproduced or transmitted
in any form or by any means, electronic or mechanical, including
photocopying, recording, or by any information storage and retrieval
system, without permission in writing from the copyright owner.

This book was printed in the United States of America

To order additional copies of this book, contact:
Xlibris Corporation
1-888-795-4274
www.Xlibris.com
Orders@Xlibris.com

97016

Contents

With Appreciation and Gratitude

To

Ken Wilber

Rev. Nonin Chowaney,
Abbot of Nebraska Zen Center

Dennis Jones

Robert Miller

Also

To the love of my life
Margot H. Treon

To my amazing and wondrous children
Annette, Jacqueline, Erik, Valerie, Areca and **Orion**

And in loving memory of my wonderful brother
Dennis Treon

Preface

This combined narrative dialogue and play is about the uncreated, unborn and undying transcendent *Self* of God-consciousness and Buddha-nature. It describes an odyssey of transcendent Consciousness Awakening and Remembrance, as viewed from transpersonal and primarily post-metaphysical Onliness Way of Enlightenment perspective.

The conversational interaction between the two characters of this book, which concerns their shared journey of transcendental Nondual Spirit-as-Spirit Consciousness Realization, is *primarily* intended to be read as a narrative dialogue. However, it is *also* created and structured in play format, and is intended to be presented to an audience as a play. And herein lies a formidable presentation problem.

As a play, it almost certainly has a *very limited* audience appeal. In relation to the current content tastes of people of a general audience, the play has no scenes of violence, gun-play, murder, fighting, battles, sex scenes, yelling, screaming, car chases, flying saucers, and no bad guys versus good guys, monsters, vampires, aliens or cyborgs. The play simply involves the quiet dialogue between two characters over a sixteen year period, set in various scenic locations.

So, speaking from the more cynical and pessimistic side of egoic self, I would say, to borrow the phrase of the burly "Mr. T" of the old TV series called "The A Team", "I pity the fool" who tries to present this play to a general audience. This would almost certainly be a disaster. On the other hand, I suspect that there is a small, or should I say *very* small, and select audience of people who would variously enjoy and appreciate this play, and derive useful meaning and insight from it.

So, speaking from the more optimistic and supportive side of egoic self, I would praise and encourage anyone, any producer, director, cast and crew, who had the courage, chutzpah, and theatrical nerve and skills to present this play to *any* audience, selective or otherwise.

Act 1, Scene 1

A man and a woman slowly walk alone, along a path together through the rolling wooded hills of mostly large oak and maple trees in southwest Wisconsin's uplands area. They appear to be quietly talking and gesturing as they walk. It is a pleasantly warm and mostly sunny day with scattered white clouds floating high above. The quiet songs and sounds of birds are in the air. They are walking along the side of one of these steep and heavily wooded hills. In awhile they stop at a rocky out-cropping along the hill, in a small and fairly level area within the secluded woods. Each sits down upon the ground on the dry leaves and grass, resting their backs on the trunks of two adjacent trees. The audience views these two face-on within this setting. The man, a teacher and professor here and there, now and then, a kind of vagabond scholar speaks:

Vagabond Scholar (VS): Supposed sage, I've come to you to see if you have anything of worth to say to me. My learned friend tells me that you do. He says that he has spoken with you many times. But I'm wondering who and what it is you claim to be?

Sage: No one special or apart.

VS: What kind of counsel and advice can I expect to hear from you? And how can it be of any value or practical use to me?

Sage: There is nothing to be *gained* or *achieved* in what I say to you. Nothing to be sought or attained.

VS: That doesn't sound very helpful to me. What then *is* the purpose of your particular counsel and advice?

Sage: It has neither *purpose* nor *goal* to be accomplished. And I have no special counsel or advice to offer you.

VS: That's a hell of a note! Of what worth to me then is any of what you have to say?

Sage: What I speak of is not easily understood, and is of itself fundamentally worthless without the *ordeal* of transcendent Recognition and Transformation so as to Reveal the transpersonal transcendental Self of which I speak. Be Aware of the *Way* in which I Teach, and how I Am with You. Pay close attention.

VS: None of this encourages me. You're said to be a sage, but I'm skeptical about such pretentious words and designations. Being a sage; what kind of ego-trip is that? And anyway, I doubt you *are* a sage.

Sage: What I am or am not is not important. *Why* is it you come to me?

(Vagabond Scholar hesitates and is silent for a moment)

VS: More and more, my life seems empty and meaningless to me. I come to you down-hearted and discouraged; full of heartache and trouble. What I seek from you is a new and *better* direction, a greater and more noble goal in life to which I can aspire.

Sage: If your despair is focused within the realm-wave consciousness of *personal* egoic suffering in life, seek psychological counseling and psychotherapy. Find a trusted and insightful psychotherapist, an ego-psychologic counselor. In this way, you can began to consciously acknowledge, re-own and re-integrate into your egoic self-structure the pre-personal and personal based neurotic *shadow* dimensions of self that, primarily due to experiences of emotional trauma, pain, dread and/or fear, you've become alienated from, and have subconsciously suppressed, denied, repressed or perhaps projected onto others. And unless such *per-personal* and *personal* subconscious shadow qualities of self can be consciously recognized, acknowledged and re-integrated into self, they can subsequently reverberate within, and pathologically disrupt, further *transpersonal* transformational spiritual development as well. But if it is *transformative* transcendental spiritual counsel and guidance you seek, then first you need to know that such seeking and pursuing is *itself* the problem. What *exactly* is it you want from me?

VS: Primarily, I need your guidance and direction toward transcendent spiritual Enlightenment. And now you say my *seeking* such direction *is* the problem. You're supposed to be the sage and teacher here, so *teach* me.

Sage: You *seek* that which You already fully *are* and have always been, and will always be. What you actually seek from me is not direction and guidance *toward* , but evasion *of* and escape *from* transcendent Realization of Enlightenment. This is your self deception.

VS: That's crazy. But if what you say were so, what then would *you* suggest I do? How in the world would I go about achieving what is called Enlightenment?

Sage: First, fully recognize that your pursuit to *achieve* and *attain* Enlightenment is your way of avoiding it.

VS: I see. Do you claim to be an Enlightened person?

Sage: No.

VS: This is not too reassuring. But if you should become my spiritual teacher and guide, how can I know, and be sure, that you will *be* there for me when I need you? How can I trust and depend on you in this way?

Sage: Here I Am. The Way I teach is the Way of Onliness Awakening to Enlightenment. If you want to learn, I Am *with* You as Your teacher at *any time* and *always*.

VS: That's a strange way to put it. Tell me, are you a spiritual guide and teacher to other people also?

Sage: There are currently four other people I ongoingly meet with individually, from time to time, and offer them transcendental spiritual guidance and teaching.

VS: So, you are a spiritual teacher then. But beyond this, *who* and *what* are you?

Sage: Choicelessly, beyond words, actions, ideas, images and conceptions, I Am Radiant Self of no self. And so are *You*, just as You are right here and now.

VS: Don't talk to me like that! You're just a human being, the same as me. Your *pretence* doesn't fool me. Your sense of who you *think* you are is false, and not impressive. I don't know why I should waste my time with you.

Sage: As a bodymind person, as a personal self, I'm certainly a mortal earth-centered human being in this impermanent world of birth and death.

VS: You do no good by telling people pretentious *fabricated* untruths about themselves; about who and how you think they are. People are *not* transcendent beings! They're fragile, unstable, vulnerable, confused, emotional and very mortal beings. *Your* words further confuse and mislead, and make them feel even *more* inadequate and worse about themselves. What kind of help is that?

Sage: The words I say seldom comfort and console, and almost always agitate and irritate the personal ego self. The way they're affecting you right now. In high vision-logic consciousness expression, all I can offer you here is *one* perspective, my perspective, a theory if you will, which I call an Onliness Way of Awakening or Enlightenment.

VS: What is this "Onliness Way" about; what does it mean?

Sage: It's a broad and diversified Path, Mode or Way of Enlightenment that similarly oriented human, human-like and non-human Beings are *predominantly* predisposed to share. There are seven other equally important Enlightenment Modes according to Onliness theory, *each* of which, like Onliness, has its own yin and yang Manifestations. These seven other Modes are yin and yang Am, Actlessness, Radiance, Emptiness, Awakening, Mystery, and Mind (see Figures 5 and 7). By way of context, character, configuration, composition, structure, temperament, experience, history, and functionality, I am predominantly predisposed to this Way of Enlightenment I call Onliness. In these same ways, other Beings are likewise predominantly predisposed to one or the other of these seven other Modes of Enlightenment, according to Onliness theory.

VS: What's the *essential* nature of Onliness theory? And of what importance is it?

Sage: It's of no *Real* or *Absolute* importance at all, but perhaps is of some relative interest and importance. It's simply a *cognitive* theory of conceptual explanation and understanding of the transcendent *Ascent*, which is Wisdom and Truth, and the immanent *Descent*, which is Care and Compassion, of transcendental Consciousness, of Spirit, of Self. Basically, Onliness is a holon-polar transpersonal post-metaphysical developmental-evolutionary conception. Onliness theory is rooted in what Aldous Huxley calls the "perennial philosophy", which ideas and ideals are shared by and underlie *all* of the great mystical spiritual traditions of the world. That is to say, this Great Chain of Being perennial philosophy includes and embraces the *common core* of transcendent Compassion and Wisdom insights and ideas that are shared by all of the great spiritual religious traditions of the world. The term "Great Chain of Being" refers to the creative development-evolvement of Ultimate Spiritual Reality, as variously described in each of these spiritual traditions, as progressing from Spirit, then stepping all the way down or *involuting*, to matter, then *evolving* to life or body, to mind, to Soul, and ultimately returning again to Spirit. But beyond this, Onliness theory attempts to *integrate* the Wisdom and Insights of *pre-modernity's* Great Chain or Nest of Being (see Figure 2 for a visual diagrammatic example of this "nesting" concept) with both *modernity's* scientific and rationality insights, and *post-modernity's* cultural-contextual and co-constructed reality understandings, as well as its interpretative, inclusive and pluralistic integral holism insights. Now that's a mouthful.

VS: It all sounds very self-important to me. Like a big ego trip. It seems to me that almost everything you say creates more confusion, unnecessary complexity, frustration, and ultimately, I think, suffering for others.

Sage: There's some significant truth in what you say. I perhaps spend too much time in my head. However, the first directional guidance on the "Eight-Fold Path of Enlightenment", according to the Buddha, is "Right View" or "Right Understanding", which is what I *attempt* to do for myself, and perhaps for others too, in the expression of Onliness theory and Way of Enlightenment.

VS: From what I've read of them, your writings about Onliness theory are difficult to read, complex, boring and long-winded.

Sage: There's also *a lot* of truth to that. But let me come back to my words that agitate and irritate, and thus cause suffering to the ego-self identity. This is unavoidable, because transcendence of the illusion of *exclusive* ego-self identity and ego consciousness necessarily involves much personal struggle, agitation, irritation, frustration and suffering.

VS: You've twisted my words to suit your purpose. What I said was that *your* words and ideas, the way you express yourself, further confuses people and make them feel even more *inadequate*, and worse about themselves. But I have another question for you about Enlightenment. What do you claim to be the *nature* of this state of transcendent Enlightenment; this state of ego-self transcendence that you speak of?

Sage: First, Enlightenment is not an achievable or possessable state of Consciousness. Indeed, Enlightenment is not even a *state* among other *states* of Consciousness. It is *all* states of Consciousness, and no specific state. In fact, Enlightenment is not an It, but rather All and None. Enlightenment is not *a* perspective but rather *All* perspectives at once, and thus no *particular* perspective. Enlightenment is Consciousness without a second or other; and in this way is *Nondual* Consciousness Realization. And Nondual Consciousness *is* Self, and only Self. In this way, Self *is* Enlightenment.

VS: You're taking me around and around in circles. None of this makes sense to me. How do I *find* and *attain* this Nondual Consciousness Realization of Enlightenment?

Sage: You can't miss It. It's Your Original and True Condition and Nature. Self of Enlightenment is how and what You *always already* Are. On how to *Awaken* to Enlightenment, the Zen Buddhist Master Joshu's counsel to a new monk goes to the very heart of it. "A monk told Joshu 'I have just entered the monastery. Please teach me.' Joshu asked: 'Have you eaten you rice porridge?' The monk replied: 'I have eaten.' Joshu said: 'Then you had better wash your bowl.' At that moment the monk was enlightened." Momon's subsequent comment on this passage called "Joshu Washes the Bowl" is: "It is too clear and so it is hard to see. A dunce once searched for fire with a lighted lantern. Had he known what fire was, He could have cooked his rice much sooner." This is from the book *Zen Flesh, Zen Bones* compiled by Paul Reps.

VS: I'm not too sure *why* what Joshu said could possibly precipitate the monk's Enlightenment. And *you* say that I can't miss the Enlightenment of Nondual Consciousness Realization, but somehow I have. The way you describe the experience of Enlightenment is *not at all* how I experience myself, or what I am. You're playing word-games with me again.

Sage: This in *not* my intention. Right Words or "Right Speech" is the third on the "Eight-Fold Path of Enlightenment" in Buddhism and is of great importance according to the Buddha, as it is to me also. You feel I'm playing games with you. What is it then you would have me do?

VS: Show me *directly* how to end pointless and meaningless existence, cruelty and suffering.

Sage: Recognition, Remembrance and Realization of Nondual Self-as-Self Consciousness Awakening.

VS: Very cute. But what is the means-whereby?

Sage: Through the wrenching, painful, and difficult *transformational* ordeal of including but *transcending* one's self-contracted narcissistic and conditioned ego life and ego consciousness.

VS: That's baloney! One's ego self is all there is; it's all we *are* and *have*. Beyond imagination and pretense, there is no other life or self. To mislead people into thinking otherwise is *folly* and *foolishness*. Humans suffer enough in their everyday lives and struggles without such *added* divine self delusions and fantasies. Practical everyday people are too busy working, cooking, cleaning, studying, eating, worrying, and struggling to live and to survive to be bothered about such transcendental silliness.

Sage: This struggle to include but transcend ego life and consciousness has to occur in conjunction with, and in addition too, the *daily* suffering, efforts, concerns and struggles that you speak of. However, Nondual Spirit-as-Spirit, which is Self-as-Self, Realization *ends* all suffering.

VS: How can such Nondual Consciousness Realization *possibly* end all suffering?

Sage: Awakening to Nondual Consciousness Self Realization does not end the pains or afflictions of human embodiment, but rather ends suffering at its *source* by ending the ego's experiences of anguish, struggle, fear, dread, rumination, anger, regret, self pity, self contraction, and self-delusion *in relation to* such pain and affliction.

VS: That's *impossible* and *unrealistic*. For starters, it's beyond human nature and capacity to do this.

Sage: Awakening to Realization of Self-as-Self , which involves inclusion but transcendence of exclusive egoic life and ego consciousness, is *very* humanly possible. Such preservation and negation of ego-self ends *all* suffering by completely ending ego-self's *responses* and *reactions* to human pain and affliction, which *is* human suffering.

VS: Your Onliness theory is Pollyanna-like in outlook, it seems to me. It views this world, and especially human beings, in an unrealistically positive and optimistic light. Goodness, truth, and beauty appear to abound and prevail almost everywhere in your theory, which is *not at all* true. How do you account in Onliness for the pervasive violence, greed and evil of human behavior in this world, and the suffering these cause?

Sage: In the *relative* consciousness of this conditioned and self-contracted *ego-centered* human world of birth and death, pervasive evil, violence, cruelty and greed, deriving from human individual and collective ignorance and delusion, certainly and frequently exists, and does *indeed* occur.

VS: But how does your Onliness perspective account for and explain the *underlying* cause or causes of such human evil, cruelty, greed, delusion, ignorance and violence?

Sage: The *relative* human evil, violence and folly of this world, and the profound and devastating suffering it causes many, if not all, earth-bound conscious Being and Entities, is a function of the current generally predominant developmental-evolutionary realm-wave level and state of individual and collective personal human consciousness.

VS: So you think that such human evil and cruelty could primarily be resolved and ended through widespread human developmental-evolutionary transcendental Consciousness Realization, which transcends but includes egoic self and ego consciousness?

Sage: Basically, *yes*. But such *transpersonal* human Consciousness development and evolution, *if* it occurs, is still only a potential, only a possibility, in my opinion.

VS: Dream on! Your Onliness theory is pure "pie in the sky". It has no scientific or even rational basis. Your "goody-goody" view of the vast majority of human beings' potential for goodness, truth and beauty is "way off the charts"; completely out of touch with reality. While people generally have *some* degree of empathy, love and affection, as well as various degrees of moral and ethical sensitivities and good intentions, in relation to at least *some* other beings, most often human beings live superficial, indifferent, vain and self-centered lives. And what's more, they *don't want* to change.

Sage: I think what you say is a *partial* truth, but not the more inclusive and deeper truth. Overall, I suspect that the ꞌevolution-development of Consciousness, of Spirit or Self, *inherently* tends toward greater and greater complexity and Consciousness inclusivity. And thus, toward the evolutionary-developmental *Recognition* of Radiant Consciousness Self of All and Every, Only and Alone. That is to say, toward Nondual Spirit-as-Spirit Consciousness Realization.

VS: Pretty words, but also pretty meaningless. As is said: "Full of sound and fury, signifying nothing." To me, your Onliness perspective sounds very self-centered and individual-self oriented. Kind of "What's in it for me?"

Sage: The Way or Tao of Onliness fully incorporates and embraces the "Bodhisattva Vow" of Buddhism, which says that under *no* circumstance will one individually take Enlightenment, one will not individually become Enlightened, until *all* sentient Being are fully Enlightened.

VS: That's going to be awhile I think. What's the *point* of all these unrealistic high ideals and rhetoric? These lofty and fantastic dreams and aspirations? The people of this overburdened, often violent and suffering world need *practical* and *scientifically* based real and rational ideas and solutions to deal with their plight and problems.

Sage: There's *much* truth to what you say about this world, and how its problems need to be addressed. However, the broad solutions you put forward are not incompatible with what I've said. Indeed, the way of your solutions tend to *supplement* and thus support the ideas and ways that I've expressed.

VS: But I think one must *first* deal with these immediate and pressing individual and communal social-cultural problems of ignorance, delusion, violence and suffering *within* the existing context of this practical down-to-earth world. And to do this through employment of rational scientifically based and empirically validated actions and solutions.

Sage: I would say more integrally, neither one nor the other *first*. One can *simultaneously* work on both of these developmental-evolutionary realm-wave levels and ways of Consciousness, and indeed concurrently on several other lines and levels of human developmental consciousness, to address these problems. It need not be first *either-or*.

VS: You previously spoke of human-like and non-human beings. Who and where are such proposed beings?

Sage: In the countless billions and billions of stars with planets in this and likely other universes, it's *highly* probable, I would say virtually certain, that there has existed and exists countless and diverse billions upon billions of other evolutionary based complex advanced Consciousness Beings, Entities and societies. And given the current level of earth-centered human developmental-evolutionary based insight and behavioral tendencies, I suspect that the many, if not most, of these human, human-like and nonhuman Beings and Entities are *far more* transcendent Consciousness advanced than earth-centered humans. Also, I suspect that the configuration, manifestation and expression of many, if not most, of such Consciousness Beings and Entities, if perceptible at all, would appear *extremely* strange to us, as we humans now consciously perceive, exist and manifest today.

VS: You're a very *strange* person. If it turns out we can't even perceive them, what would be the point of it?

Sage: Them are We; They are Us. You and I *are*, as *each* of these Beings is, this Nondual Realization Self of *Mystery,* Openly and Freely arising as the entire Radiant Kosmos - infinitely, boundlessly, timelessly.

VS: How in the world does this happen? And if it's so, how would that *help* me, or make my life better?

Sage: It doesn't happen, It always already *Is*. Such transpersonal Nondual Consciousness Realization includes but *transcends* your conditioned and self-contracted personal ego bodymind feelings, ideas and concerns. Nondual Realization Self-as-Self is prior to, and thus beyond, the sequential happenings of time; is uncreated, unconditioned, uncontracted, unknowable.

VS: Unknowable? Then how come you seem to know so much about it?

Sage: I *don't* and *cannot*, because I speak to you now from only *one* perspective. It's called an advanced vision-logic ego consciousness perspective. What can be conveyed from any one perspective, especially an ego-based perspective, is very limited indeed.

VS: Almost everything you say to me is put in abstract conceptual terms. It's all very vague, obscure and impersonal. I seek and need *forgiveness* and *redemption* for myself *as a person*. One who has done things I'm ashamed of in my life, and has emotionally deeply hurt other people.

Sage: The Compassion of Forgiveness, and thus Redemption, *starts* with your own forgiveness of yourself; with Loving Kindness toward and patience with your own bodymind ego-self and consciousness. And necessary to such self forgiveness, indeed integral to it, is real and appropriate self atonement and amends. If at all possible, attempt such atonement and amends in relation to the person or people most directly involved and affected by the pain and hurt that you have caused. And at some point you need to *directly* ask someone you have harmed for his or her forgiveness. If this isn't possible, then you need to effect real and appropriate atonement and amends to earth-centered humanity in general and overall. In my view, without such authentic atonement and amends there can't be complete and total self forgiveness. In this way, self forgiveness in conjunction with atonement and amends is *basic* to the transcendental Realization of Compassion and Forgiveness toward all Beings and Entities.

VS: This is all much easier said than done. How do I specifically go about such self forgiveness, atonement and amends, so as to help establish the basis for compassion toward all beings?

Sage: In large part, through the sometimes joyful but often difficult and painful ordeal of a sustained *integral transcendental spiritual practice,* which includes self inquiry, self discipline and self application of the kind we just discussed. Also, such a practice may well include intensive personal-egoic consciousness counseling and psychotherapy. There's no *easy* answer or quick fix in relation to your question.

VS: Operationally, what's the basis of and what's involved in such an integral transcendental spiritual practice?

Sage: In the Way of Onliness, the manifest Form and unmanifest Emptiness Consciousness of Wisdom, Compassion and Communion are the three broad bases and means-whereby of such a practice. Thus embracing and applying both the transcendent Form and Emptiness Faces of *Compassion, Wisdom* and *Communion,* there are two *pragmatic* paths You need to follow so as to developmentally Recognize, Remember, and Realize transpersonal Nondual Self-as-Self Consciousness Awakening. The first path is through a disciplined and sustained *contemplative-meditative* practice; hopefully within a supportive community and with guidance from an experienced teacher of that meditative-contemplative perspective. The second path is through a disciplined and sustained study-therapy-exercise-practice-application *in* daily life of at least the following developmental lines of personal self. These lines of development include *cognitive*, like aesthetic, analytic, literary, philosophic, scientific and so on, *affective-emotional-sexual*, *physiologic*, as in your physical body, *interpersonal-relational-social-ethical-moral-cultural-environmental*, and finally *transpersonal-spiritual* developmental lines. That is, an *integral practice* that simultaneously includes individual work toward development of body, emotion, mind, Soul and Spirit in all three domains of personal, social-communal-cultural, and nature-environmental or physical reality.

VS: But what kinds of direction and guidance do I need on these two developmental paths of Enlightenment, that include these issues of Compassion, Wisdom and Communion; which *you* suggest will play an important part in my personal forgiveness, atonement and redemption?

Sage: On these two paths of practice be guided, broadly speaking, by your own co-created and co-enacted *goodness*, leading toward that which is Good; *truthfulness*, leading toward that which is True; and *beauty*, leading toward that which is Beautiful.

VS: That's no help at all! You frustrate me at every turn. I understand what you say, but such a statement leads me *nowhere*. Most of what you tell me is empty, abstract and without specific meaningful substance.

(Motionless and without expression, Sage sits in silence for a while.)

VS: You say that I'm already a fully Awakened and Enlightened being, *then* you tell me what a difficult and painful struggle and ordeal it will be to realize this *same* Enlightenment. Which is it?

Sage: Both. You already deeply *Understand* and *Know* that You are unborn and undying Divine Self of Consciousness. This Liberation and Freedom Self of Bliss. But in delusion and ignorance, you refuse to transcendentally See and Acknowledge this.

VS: This is simply *not* true!

This scene slowly darkens, and fades from view into blackness.

Act 1, Scene 2

Sage and Vagabond Scholar slowly walk together on the grass across the mall, and then seat themselves next to one another among the scattered oak trees on the grassy mall of the east bank University of Minnesota-Minneapolis campus. Students sit around and walk by them in the background. Also in the audience's background view are the neo-classical columned academic buildings, including Northrup Auditorium. It is a warm and sunny early fall afternoon. Each has a paper sack lunch with them and they share a canteen containing water. They leisurely eat their sandwiches, corn chips and pieces of fruit, and drink from their canteen of water as they talk. The quiet background sounds of birds and people talking are in the air.

Sage: I want you to ongoingly immerse yourself in reading and study as a *condition* of my being your spiritual teacher and guide. As long as I am your teacher, it is *required* that you continuously gain knowledge and understanding through in-depth reading and study of all of the great mystical spiritual traditions of the world; certainly including those of Buddhism, Hinduism, Christianity, Islam, Judaism, and the Baha'i Faith also. But your continuing reading and study must also and *equally* include the writing of the numerous and great transcendental spiritual sages, adepts and philosophers, past and present, who have written so insightfully about transcendental and transpersonal Consciousness and Awakening. And in the present, certainly the profound and insightful writings of the contemporary philosopher Ken Wilber should be carefully studied. In this same way, and *equally* importantly, you must complete ongoing and extensive readings and study in all of the physical and social sciences, all of the arts, literature, poetry, and in cultural studies and the humanities;

including readings and study in pre-modern, modern, and post-modern perspectives and philosophy. In other words, you have an extensive reading and study assignment ahead of you.

VS: I love to read and study, so this sounds good to me. I will do it. But if I'm to become your student and you my transcendental spiritual teacher and guide, is there any financial or other kinds of costs or obligations you require of me, beyond what you've just said?

Sage: No, absolutely not. Such a relationship, in my view, cannot and must not, directly or indirectly, involve *any type* of financial or any other kinds of material costs, exchange, obligation, advantage, or benefit in relation to either student or spiritual teacher and guide.

VS: I understand. However, I do have some concern about this Nondual Consciousness transcendental Self you say I always and already am. This makes no rational sense to me. The *whole* transcendent thing you talk about lacks reason and logic. It seems to me a kind of illogical and primitive *magical* or imaginary way of thinking and speaking.

Sage: I will often speak to you in a non-logical manner, but don't confuse pre-logical with trans-logical thought. What I tell you about transpersonal Self Awakening is often trans-logical in nature. It includes but *transcends* the content of co-constructed reason and logic worldspace consciousness. Because what I say to you may be non-logical does not mean it is pre-logical. As the philosopher Ken Wilber points out, non-logical content may be either *pre-logical* expressions of archaic, magic or mythic realm-wave consciousness, or *trans-logical* expressions of transcendental realm-wave Consciousness, and to mis-identify and confound these two worldspace realm-waves of Consciousness creates *much* confusion.

VS: You always have some fancy and tricky answer for me, don't you. It's lucky you have people like Ken Wilber to fall back on for your ideas.

Sage: Yes it is.

VS: When you say that I always and already am this transcendental Self of Enlightenment do you mean that I'm a *part* of this transcendent Self; or perhaps a *partial* manifestation or expression of Self?

Sage: No. It means that You always and already, here and now, are the whole, only, and all of Nondual Self-as-Self Consciousness Enlightenment Itself. You are neither a *part* or *reflection* of Spirit-as-Spirit Awakening, nor a *partial* or *potential* gesture or expression of transcendent Self-as-Self Realization. Rather, You are, and indeed each and every Consciousness Entity is, the *full* and *complete* Actualization and Realization of Nondual Self-as-Self Consciousness Awakening - Only and Alone. You are this Divine Self of Enlightenment Itself, fully, completely, and none other Than.

VS: I understand. I've been wondering what you meant during our first meeting in reference to the manifest Form and unmanifest Emptiness Consciousness of transcendental Ultimate Reality.

Sage: Manifest Form, which in Onliness is called *Being* Consciousness, and unmanifest Emptiness, called *Nonbeing* Consciousness in Onliness, are the two holon-polar transcendental Sides or Faces of Ultimate Reality or Self, *as viewed* from high vision-logic personal consciousness, and also from certain realm-waves of transpersonal Consciousness. It is within manifest *Form* Consciousness that Samsara finds expression. Samsara is the manifest world of struggle, suffering, sorrow, birth and death. It is within unmanifest *Emptiness* Consciousness that Nirvana is Realized. Nirvana is the Liberation from and cessation of all manifest struggle, suffering, sorrow, birth and death.

VS: That's very general and kind of confusing. What specifically do you mean by transcendent Form or Being Consciousness, and Emptiness or Nonbeing Consciousness?

Sage: From high vision-logic consciousness point of view, in transcendent *manifest* Reality the realm-wave of Being Consciousness is the open and abundant Fullness of Spirit's or Self's Abyss of *every changing, configurative* and *evolving* Form. Likewise, in transcendent *unmanifest* Reality the realm-wave of Nonbeing Consciousness is the open and abundant Freedom of Spirit's or Self's Abyss of *ever changeless, timeless* and *formless* Emptiness. But also remember that in Reality Itself, which is Self-as-Self, Form *is* Emptiness; Emptiness *is* Form. Samsara is Nirvana; Nirvana is Samsara. They are One and the Same.

VS: So, more double-talk.

(Sage laughs and Vagabond Scholar smiles also.)

VS: The ideas of Form and Emptiness, Samsara and Nirvana, may be interesting conceptual abstractions, but what, if anything, is the significance and practical implications of such ideas?

Sage: One implication, as the philosopher Ken Wilber points out, is that, since Enlightenment can be defined as transcendent Consciousness that *includes* and *expresses* Realization of all manifest Form and of all unmanifest Emptiness, the meaning and content of Enlightenment itself cannot be *fixed* and *unchanging* since Form is not fixed and unchanging, but rather ever changing and evolving. Thus human Enlightenment must be defined *in relation to* the historical era in which it occurs. That is, in the Ascent-Descent of Spirit, the *relative* meaning and content of an individual's Enlightenment includes and expresses *only* all of the manifest Forms that have evolved *up to* a given point in historical time.

VS: Is Nondual Self-as-Self Consciousness Enlightenment then a holon that is transcended but included like all the other holons that precede it, and are parts within and under it?

Sage: Onliness theory asserts that this additional and more consciousness-inclusive *relative* knowledge and meaning that is a function of human historical development-evolution does not create a new *transcendental* whole and unique holonic shift; is not a transcendently *transformed* new and unique holon of Nondual Self-as-Self Consciousness Realization. Rather, it is only a *translational* shift of *relative* knowledge within Absolute Self Reality Enlightenment. Nondual Self Reality Awakening transcends but includes all holons below It, but is not Itself transcendentally transformed; is *not* Itself transcended but included as a part of yet a more Consciousness inclusive holon, and in this way is not Itself a holon. So, Nondual Consciousness of Self Reality is *trans-holonic* in Nature, in that it is neither holonic nor is it not holonic, and both.

VS: That's all remarkably remote, but of some philosophical interest. But this is merely abstract conceptual speculation. Tell me something I can *use* right now. Like if I were to practice meditation, what's the best way to do it?

Sage: Consult books at the library or go to the internet on the various ways of meditation-contemplation; or talk with others you trust about how they meditate or contemplate. There are several effective ways to practice meditation and contemplation. Based on my own temperament and experiences, I prefer a variation of what's called in Zen Buddhism "serene reflection meditation". In this, without tension or special effort, I sit facing a blank wall, seated on a small firm pillow with my neck and back relaxed but aligned straight and upright, my chin tucked slightly in with the top and back of my head directed toward the ceiling, and my knees bent in a cross-legged sitting position. If need be, you can also sit in a chair or even walk slowly, and still do this kind of meditation. My eyes are mostly opened, but maybe closed or partially opened, and I look forward at the wall. My hands rest upon my lap with fingers of one hand partially overlapping the finger of the other, and my thumb tips resting against each other so as to form a kind of ring, which ring is centered just below my belly button area. I let ideas, thoughts, feelings, sensations and images arise and pass; neither holding on to them nor pushing them away. When my mind wanders, I bring it back to this open, awake, calm and quiet state of Emptiness; or, to bring mind back to Emptiness, I might focus my attention *solely* on the actual physical experience and sensations of breathing each breath as it naturally occurs. One can sit zazen, as it's called, like this for short and long periods of time. In sitting zazen I'm not trying to do, accomplish, achieve or attain anything at all. Such meditation is simply an end *in* and *of* itself.

VS: That's all there is to it?

Sage: Basically, yes.

VS: Such meditation appears to me like I'm idly sitting around and wasting the limited time I have in life; staring blankly at a blank wall and accomplishing *nothing*.

Sage: At a minimum however, whatever meditation-contemplation you may chose, *if* you do it diligently and mindfully, you can *directly* experience and empirically test for yourself whether such meditation-contemplation facilitates, has no effect upon, or interferes with and retards your own transcendental spiritual growth and development.

VS: You say that meditation is an *end* in and of itself. But isn't the purpose and goal of meditation-contemplation to awaken to, achieve, and thus attain Enlightenment?

Sage: No. In this very moment You always, already *are* fully and completely Enlightened, just as You are here and now. You *are* Self, and Self *is* Enlightenment only. You are, and always have been, this Spirit; this Divine Self of Awakened transcendent Consciousness. But your ego self and consciousness refuses to Confess and Acknowledge This.

VS: Why does my ego self, or should I say "I", refuse such confession and acknowledgment?

Sage: As I've suggested, as exclusive ego self identity you are mired and entangled in this self-centered consciousness of illusion, ignorance and delusion, and thus can't *Recognize* and *See* your complete identification with, and entanglement in, this narcissistic egoic worldspace consciousness; or indeed See anything *beyond* it.

VS: How then did I get so entangled in it?

Sage: As an earth-centered human being you were conceived and born with this *potential* for subsequent development into this realm-wave level and state of ego-centered co-created worldspace consciousness. In daily life it's the highest consciousness you've been exposed to, surrounded by and immersed in, and have immersed yourself in; the one you've predominantly experienced, recognized, known and been conditioned by. In fact, as you've said, it's the highest and only worldspace consciousness you think there *is*.

VS: Then meditation helps you to become more awake and alert to your conditioning *by,* and immersion *in,* this egoic worldspace consciousness?

Sage: Yes. But understand that meditation is one manifest *Form* of Awakening and Enlightenment Itself, and thus is an end in and of itself, and has no goal or purpose *beyond* itself.

VS: I see. Why is it you sometimes talk of "co-created" or "co-constructed worldspaces" of consciousness?

Sage: Post-modernism point out that for humans at least, and perhaps for other conscious Beings, reality, at any given moment, is literally co-constructed through a *synthesis* of an individual's *interpretation* of their interior and subjective and inter-subjective perceptual worldspace consciousness of conceptions, understandings, insights, visions and realizations *interacting with* that individual's perceptual sensory *interpretation* of their exterior and objective and inter-objective worldspace consciousness, of what are nominally called objects, actions and processes. Thus, for a such a consciousness Entity there exists no single *separately objective* and independently existing world of exterior reality waiting to be discovered that is *beyond* or *outside* of one's own *projected perceptual interpretations* of it. I am simply acknowledging the important relative truth of this insight.

VS: So, through this interpretative synthesis, each and every consciousness being has its own distinct and separate projected worldspace consciousness reality. And for that conscious entity, this is its real and true *fundamental* reality?

Sage: Yes. And the content or form of this reality continuously changes, constantly develops and evolves, in each and every moment.

VS: How do you define and identify a "consciousness entity"? And how many could there be?

Sage: *All* is Consciousness, None other than. Self or Spirit *is* Consciousness only, without a second or opposite. Thus all "things" or "entities" in all worlds and universes are this Divinity of Consciousness; that is to say, are transcendental Self-as-Self. And You are, *here* and *now*, this Self of All and None, Many and One.

VS: You're driving me crazy! I feel like I'm on a merry-go-round that I can't get off of, because it never stops. So, for conscious beings, manifest reality is protectively co-constructed, co-created and co-enacted, and is not just externally and objectively *out there* for us to see and discover.

Sage: I think postmodernism is correct in this regard. However, Onliness theory asserts that this is true *only* up to developmental-evolutionary Nondual Self-as-Self Consciousness Realization; only up to Self of Absolute Reality. As Enlightened Buddha-mind Self of God-consciousness, postmodernism's co-constructed, co-created and co-enacted interpretative, pluralistic and cultural-contextual influences and insights are *transcended* but included, negated and preserved; and thus no longer inherently arise or occur in Consciousness. Nondual Realization Self of Consciousness is *both* subject and object, and neither. It has no *separate* other-ness, thing-ness or plural-ness about It to *be* interpreted, and yet is plural also - Many and One, and also None. It has no context, as It *is* each and all contexts at once, and None. As I said, It is *at once* both the Interpreter, or Subject, and the Interpreted, or Object; and Neither. Also, and aside from this topic, keep in mind that, as Buddhism points out, *all* of manifest Reality is impermanent; all of its co-constructed forms must arise and pass away. Unchangingly then, for the phenomena of manifest Reality there is *only* the impermanence of change.

VS: You're giving me a headache. What then, if anything, is permanent?

Sage: Permanence implies the relative realm-wave of time. In this temporal context, the presence of Self is permanent, indeed *is* Permanence Itself. However, beyond time and timelessness, beyond permanence and impermanence, remember that *You* are this transcendent Self of Truth.

VS: Why do you say such a thing to me?

Sage: Because it's True.

VS: Are you including my everyday bodymind ego-self when you say that about me?

Sage: Yes, because it *too* is Self, and none other Than.

VS: But you always speak very negatively about ego self and ego consciousness; putting it down and telling me that ego self needs to be overcome and transcended.

Sage: The consciousness of ego self is *critically* important, indeed indispensable, to the effective negotiation, functioning and well being of bodymind within the everyday social and physical world of birth and death. Thus ego self must be protected, maintained, nurtured and developed in this regard. However, the consciousness level of ego self-sense must also be *transcended* but included, negated and preserved, at higher transpersonal, trans-egoic realm-wave levels and states of developmental-evolutionary Consciousness. But indeed, manifest Beings must continue to monitor, develop and evolve ego self and consciousness even up to, and into, Nondual Self-as-Self, that is Spirit-as-Spirit, Realization Consciousness.

VS: I see. The problem is, I already know too well how to *include* ego self as primary and central to my life, but how do I *transcend* it?

Sage: This involves a moment to moment and day by day formidable, persistent and ongoing struggle. Your *exclusive* identification with egoic consciousness, as egoic self, is highly conditioned and *deeply* rooted, and almost always hidden from your view and consciousness.

VS: How can I uproot it and bring it into view?

Sage: Through your Kosmocentric integral transcendental spiritual practice *in, of, with* and ultimately *as* the World, and *as* all Worlds.

VS: How do I dis-identify from egoic self-sense without destroying it? In the process of such dis-identification, how is it possibly to avoid destroying this personal ego-consciousness *I am,* and know *so* well?

Sage: The "how" is usually slowly and carefully. And doing so by *Observing, Unwrapping* and *Revealing* the true nature, character and functioning of your moment to moment and day by day ego life and self. And certainly with guidance and help from others who are making, or have made, this difficult and often painful journey.

VS: But how does this *happen*?

Sage: In the course your integral transcendental spiritual practice, as you gradually become Aware of, Realize, and Experience higher transpersonal states of Consciousness, *use* such higher states to

Observe and Recognize the *functioning* and *character* of your egoic consciousness, but *now* from the perspective of these higher transcendent states of Consciousness. This transpersonal Recognition and Realization of the nature of ego self-sense identity and functioning will progressively help you to objectify, differentiate from, and gradually *dis-identify* with your exclusive ego self and ego consciousness identity.

VS: What kinds of *functions* would I look for in my ego self-sense consciousness; what would I see and find there?

Sage: Along with the many effective navigating and negotiating strengths and advantages of ego function consciousness in this everyday temporal world of birth and death, You would see the very *narrow* range and *limited* view of Consciousness that ego self affords. And in this context you would also observe the blind, cruel and destructive problems and issues that arise as a function of exclusive egoic self identity and consciousness.

VS: What kinds of problems and issues derive from, or arise at, this realm-wave level and state of egoic self-sense consciousness?

Sage: For me, to mention just a few, these problematic and destructive egoic issues include self-importance, selfishness, anger, impatience, excessive ego-defensiveness, aggressiveness, and over-controllingness at times; as well as cruelty, self delusion, ignorance, hate, indifference, complaining and criticizing, pettiness, pretentiousness, arrogance, deception-evasion, jealousy, envy, avarice and greed, stinginess, resentment, unforgivingness, self-conceit, self-centeredness, self-indulgence. All of which of course are *also* Self and Self only. These are developmental-evolutionary aspects of *pre-egoic* and *pre-personal* as well as *personal egoic* realm-wave stages and states of consciousness that need to be addressed, both at egoic levels, in psychotherapy for example, as well as Observed and Recognized from the vantage point of trans-egoic, transpersonal levels of Consciousness, so as to be acknowledged, re-integrated and resolved. And thus included but *transcended* in the developmental-evolutionary transpersonal Ascent-Descent of

Self.

VS: You may be even *more* messed up than I am. So is this right? I observe, recognize and acknowledge all aspects of my egoic life and consciousness *from within* these higher transcendent states of Consciousness, and in this way I'm able to *reconcile, include* and *re-integrate* my egoic self within and into these higher states, and thus include but transcend exclusive egoic life and consciousness?

Sage: Yes. And each higher and more Consciousness inclusive realm-wave state and stage of developmental-evolutionary Consciousness reveals a broader and deeper Vision and Realization of Reality, of Self. Yet each such higher state and stage still includes all realm-waves that have preceded it, but *now* they're *Seen* and *Comprehended* from the point of view of this new and more Consciousness-inclusive stage and state transcendent Self Reality.

VS: In a way, this kind of discourages me. I think of how *far* I have to go in my own development, and how difficult and disruptive this development will be. Who needs all that prolonged developmental effort, turmoil and confusion?

Sage: Vagabond Scholar, You *are* this unborn and undying Divine Self of always already Buddha-mind Enlightenment, right here and now.

The scene slowly darkens and fades from view into blackness.

Act 1, Scene 3

Sage and Vagabond Scholar are seated alone on folding chairs next to and partially facing one another on a large wooden deck. This deck is on a hill with surrounding large oak, basswood and pine trees all around. Just to the side and partially in front of them, close by and in clear view, is a Minnesota sky blue lake that ripples and glistens in the sunlight. This hill and deck overlook the lake and the woods that can be seen in the distance beyond the lake, on the other side. It is a warm and mostly sunny mid-morning with a slight breeze, and some large white clouds float in the sky. The quiet sounds of bird songs fill the air. The audience views these two mostly face-on, with the surrounding trees and lake also in the audience's view beyond them.

VS: You sometimes speak of "realm-waves" and I'm not sure what you mean by this term?

Sage: The expressions *realm-wave stage* or *realm-wave level* versus *realm-wave state* are the two concepts that you need to differentiate. First, the "realm" in "realm-wave" expresses the *outside-objective awareness* nature and perspective of that level or stage and state of consciousness a Being is ongoingly and stably at in their development-evolution. Conversely, the word "wave" in "realm-wave" expresses the *inside-subjective experiential* nature and perspective of the level or stage and state of consciousness a Being is ongoingly and stably at in their development-evolution. Unless otherwise specified, the term "realm-wave" by itself implies *both* a given ongoing and stable developmental-evolutionary *stage* or *level* of consciousness a Being is at, *and* the associated ongoing and stable *state* of consciousness that is inherent to that stage or level of consciousness. Also, a Being may have transitionally developed to a given realm-wave *level* and *state* of consciousness but not yet ongoingly and stably so, in which case that Being will likely experience *temporary* or *fleeting states* of consciousness characteristic of and inherent to that new realm-wave *stage* or *level*. Finally, as the philosopher Ken Wilber points out, any realm-wave *state* of consciousness, even the highest transcendental states of Consciousness, can temporarily or fleetingly occur at any given realm-wave *stage* or *level* of consciousness an individual is at, high or low. However, that temporary state of consciousness will always be interpreted *through* and understood *at* the degree of consciousness-inclusiveness screen characteristic of and inherent to the *stage* or *level* that the individual is currently stably at. Thus, it needs to be recognized that there are also *temporary* or *fleeting* realm-wave *states* of Consciousness that sometimes must to be designated.

VS: I understand. Sage, I began a practice of daily half-hour to one hour meditation periods shortly after our second meeting, primarily using the serene reflection meditation approach that you described.

Sage: How is that going?

VS: It's kind of interesting, but my mind wanders off a lot; thinking about everyday "this and that" events and happenings. Mostly rehearsing upcoming and rehashing past events. I keep trying to "just sit and just look" as you said, letting feelings, thoughts, sensations and images arise and pass, but it's hard to do. Focusing all my attention *only* on my breathing does seem to help stop mind-wandering, for a while at least.

Sage: Sounds like you're doing well. But where can mind wander that is *beyond* or outside of Self, since there is no "outside" *to* Self?

VS: Very droll, I'm sure. But it's hard to sit in this way, even for half an hour. After awhile my knees began to hurt, and my legs "go to sleep" and get kind of numb. I get sleepy too and start to fall asleep sometimes.

Sage: Stay quietly alert and awake in meditation. Over time, your aches and pains will gradually fade into the background of consciousness and essentially subside.

VS: You're right, I'm noticing my aches and pains are disappearing more and more. But I don't notice any change or difference in myself since I started meditation.

Sage: That sometimes takes twenty or more years of meditation practice.

VS: Jesus! Twenty years! I can't do this for twenty years in the *hope* I might then see some development toward my Enlightenment.

Sage: It's not *your* Enlightenment. It doesn't and cannot belong to you. It's not a *thing* that you can own. Indeed, Enlightenment, which *is* Nondual Self-as-Self Awakening, has neither *it-ness*, that is, particularity, nor *of-ness*, that is part-ness or partiality.

VS: I don't know what the last thing you said about of-ness, part-ness or partiality means.

Sage: I think you do.

VS: Talking to you is like wandering in an endless "house of mirrors". The farther in I go the more puzzled, confused and disoriented I become.

Sage: Don't confuse yourself. Recall that meditation practice is not done to reach goals. In meditation, it's possible to observe ego consciousness and functioning; how you use ego self to effectively function, as well as how it can be used to confuse, delude and blind yourself in life. See egoic self and consciousness for how and what it *is*.

VS: I realized recently that, like you, I too seem to be predominantly predisposed by temperament and experience to what you call the holon-polar Onliness Way or Mode of Enlightenment, as opposed to one of the other seven Enlightenment Modes you've described in Onliness theory. I'm talking about the other holon-polar Enlightenment Modes of Am, Actlessness, Radiance, Emptiness, Awakening, Mystery, and Mind (see Figure 5 and 7). What do *you* think?

Sage: I think you're right. You *are* predominantly predisposed in this way.

VS: But what exactly does being predominantly predisposed to Oniliness *mean*?

Sage: (Removing five paper diagrams from her pocket, Sage unfolds and spreads the diagrams (Figures 3, 4, 5, 6 and 7) out on the small table between them, and then, in turn, points to each realm-wave and Mode of Consciousness listed in these diagrams while speaking about their respective contents) First, understand that *all* human beings, irrespective of which of the eight Enlightenment Modes they are predisposed to, are predominantly predisposed to the *Soul*-Consciousness Realization of *Psychic Multi-istence's* diverse beings realm-wave of *Pan-gnostic Existence* Awareness and Experience (pointing to Figures 3, 4, 6 and 7; and then comparing Figures 3, 4 and 5). Those Beings within Pan-gnostic Existence Awareness and Experience, like You and I, who are predominantly predisposed to the Oniliness Mode or Way of Enlightenment are, in turn, predisposed toward transpersonal *Compassion* Experience and *Knowledge* Awareness, and *within* these We are predisposed toward *Righteousness* Experience and *Intuition* Awareness, so as to guide and facilitate Our Ascent-Descent of Self Awakening and Realization (pointing to these realm-waves in Figure 5 in relation to their derivation and termination relative to yin and yang Oniliness). To guide and facilitate Our Ascent-Descent of Self in *subsequent* transpersonal development, We now transcend but include these same Oniliness related predispositions just described *into* and *within* the transcendent *Soul*-Consciousness Realization realm-wave of *universive* Subtle Prim-istence's Pan-gnostic Existence Consciousness (pointing to Figure 4); to which Consciousness We are initially predominantly predisposed, but which developmentally merges toward Trans-gnostic Existence Consciousness, and ultimately resolves into Existence Being's Consciousness at this realm-wave's culmination. With the subsequent transcendent Realization of *supreme* Subtle Prim-istence realm-wave, We have some initial predisposition toward Existence Being's Consciousness, which developmentally merges toward Transexistence Being's Consciousness, and ultimately resolves into Being's manifest Form Consciousness at this realm-wave's culmination. And within subsequent Realization of *absolute* Subtle Holistent Prim-istence realm-wave Consciousness, We have some initial predisposition toward Being's manifest Form Consciousness as It developmentally merges toward the ultimate integrated resolution of Being's manifest Form and Nonbeing's unmanifest Emptiness Consciousness, at the culmination of this realm-wave; and the subsequent emergence of Causal Holistence Consciousness (pointing to Figures 4, 6 and 7). And thus, with the Realization of *absolute* Holistent Prim-istence realm-wave Consciousness, at its culmination, there developmentally occurs the remarkable *transcendence* but inclusion, and thus resolution, of the predisposition distinction between Being's Form and Nonbeing's Emptiness Consciousness, *as well as* the *transcendence* but inclusion, and thus *dissolution*, of the *differential* predisposition tendency toward any one or the other of the eight Modes of Enlightenment; that is, for You and I, the dissolution of Our predisposition toward Onliness Mode of Enlightenment Itself. At the culmination of *absolute* Subtle Holistent Prim-istence then, there occurs only an equally balanced predisposition toward all eight Modes of Enlightenment, and thus these singularly-focused *predominant predisposition* Mode distinctions no longer arise or occur in Consciousness. (Figures 4, 6 and 7).

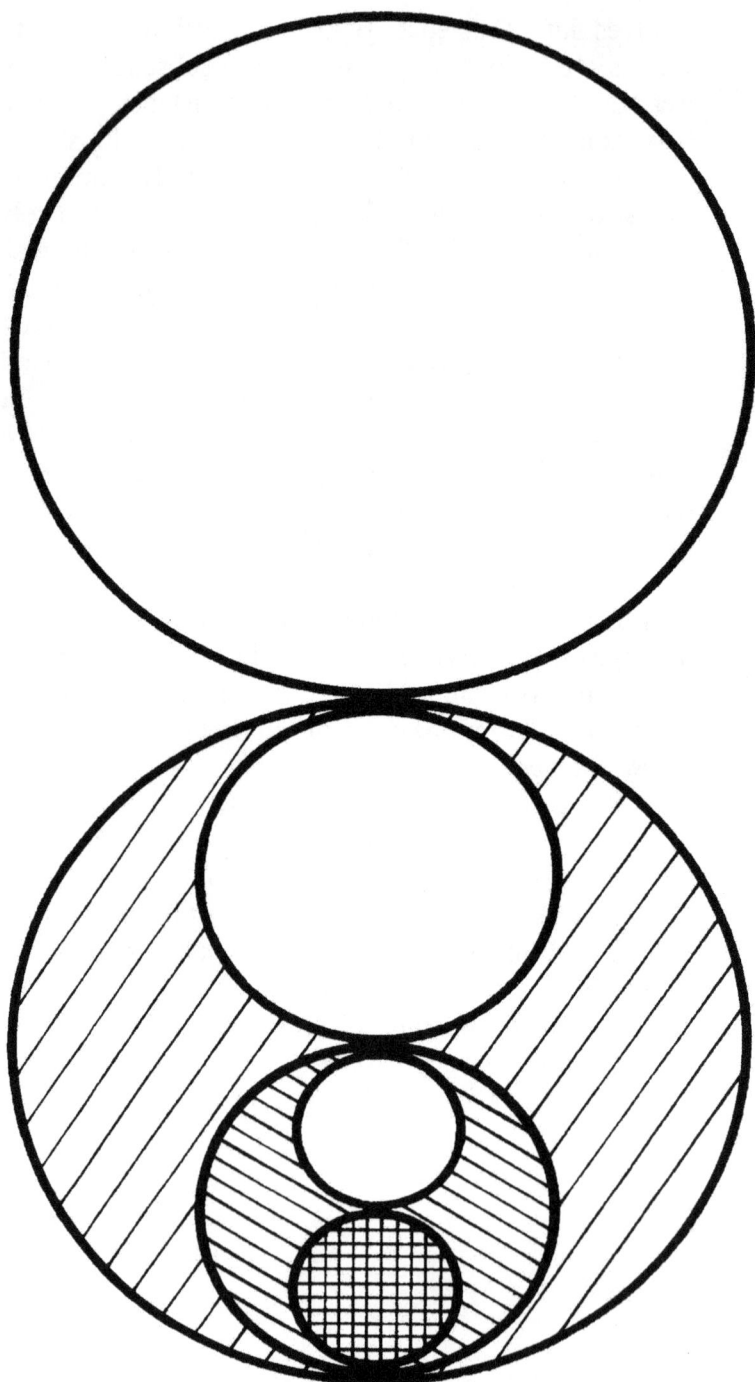

FIGURE 1

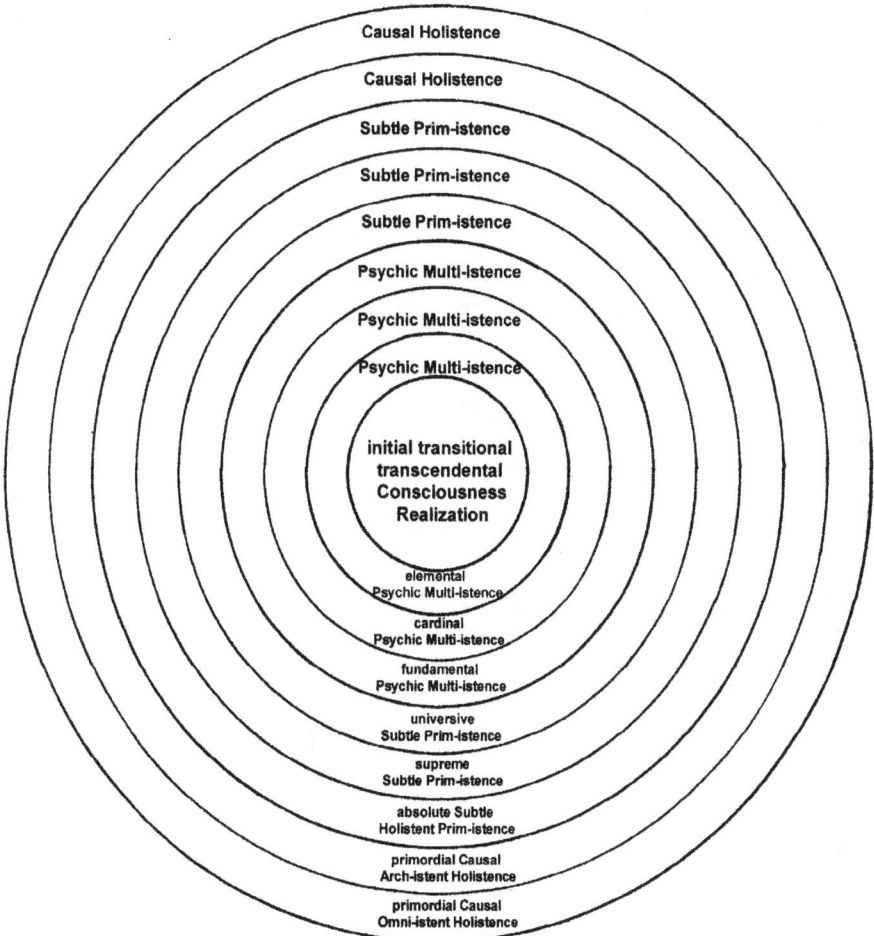

Holonic-concept diagram (i.e., holon-only versus integrated holon-polar diagram) of the developmental-evolutionary Ascent-Descent of transcendental Consciousness in Onliness theory and perspective.

FIGURE 2

40

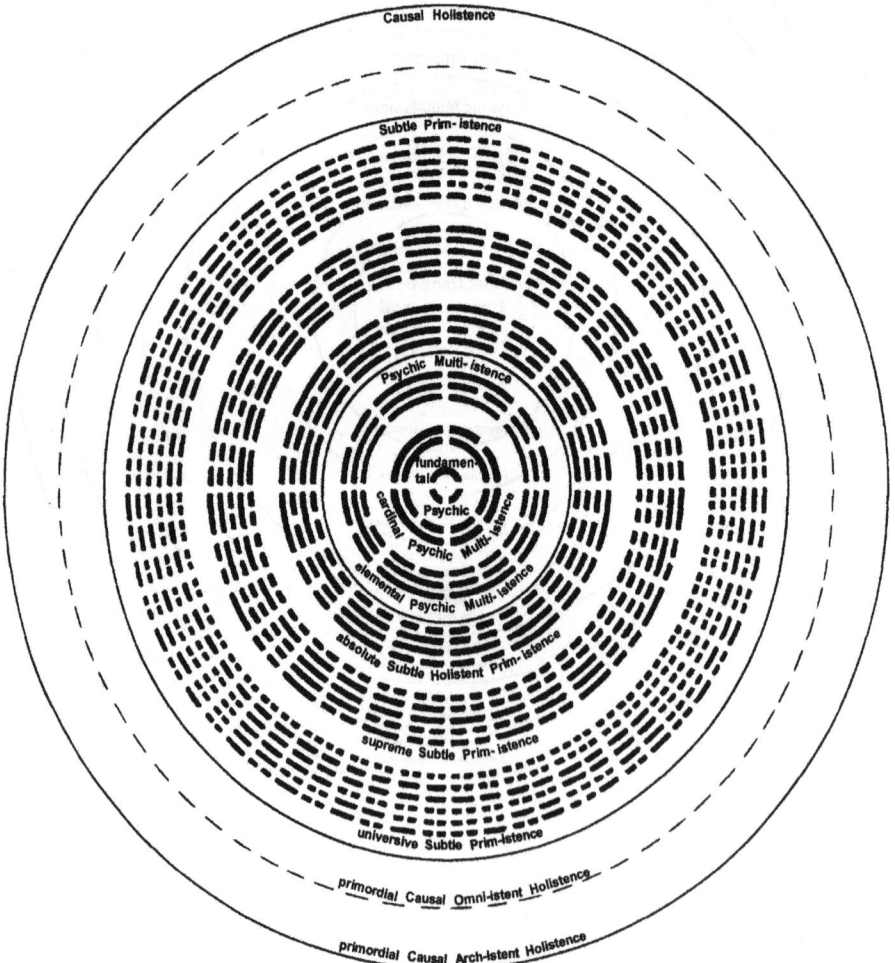

FIGURE 3

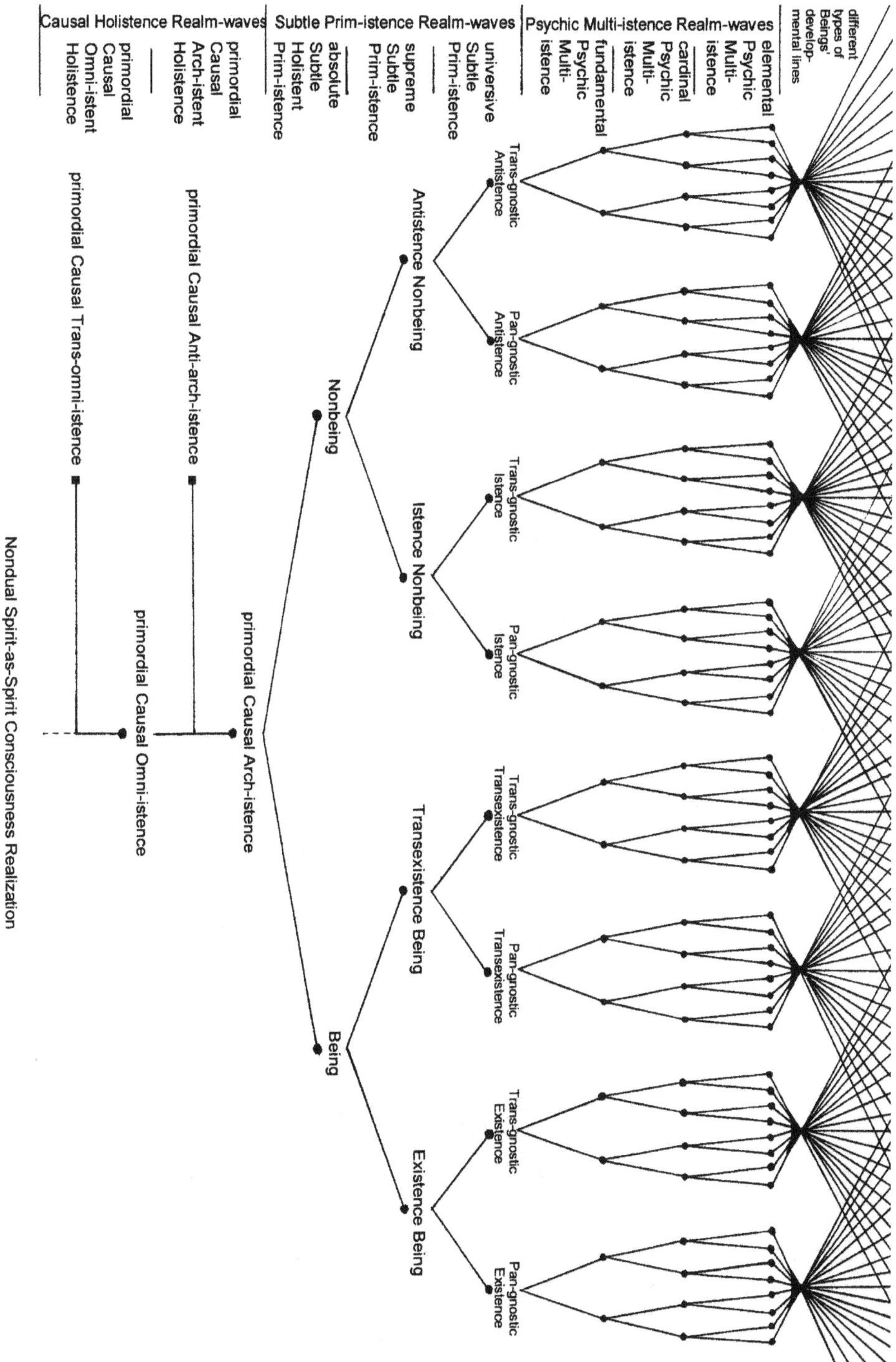

FIGURE 4

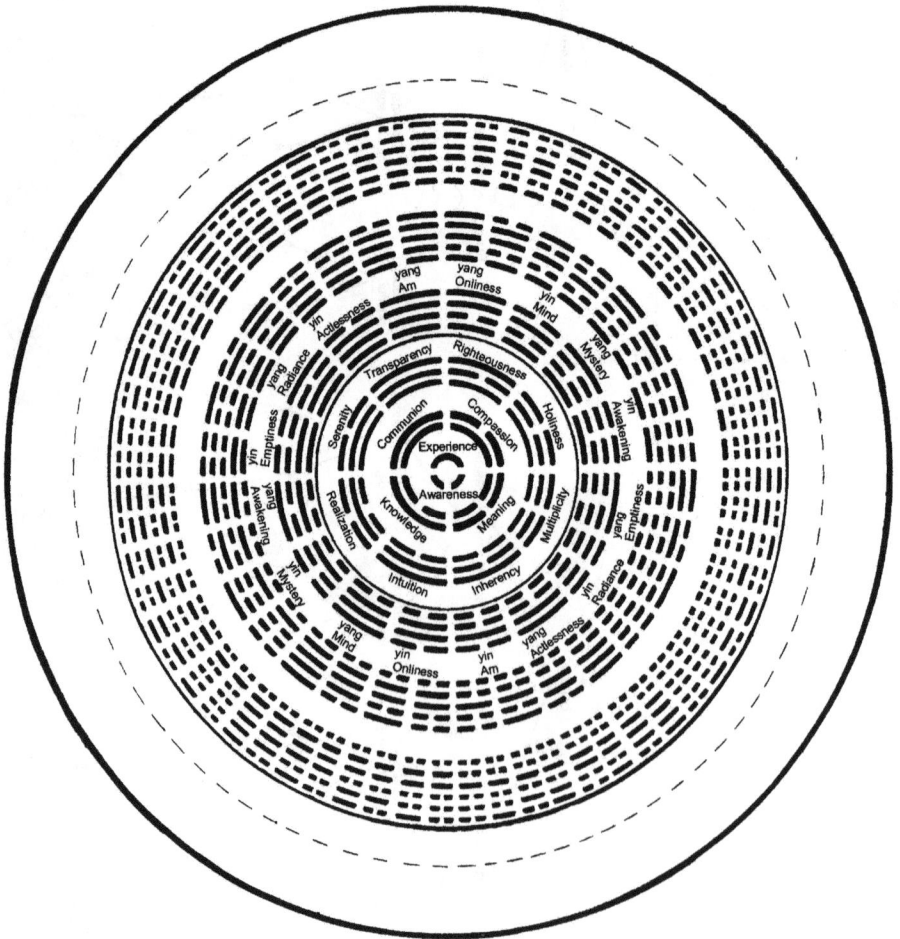

FIGURE 5

Different types of human and human-like beings' developmental-evolutionary lines		
Initial transitional transcendental Consciousness Realization		

Psychic Pan-gnostic Existence	elemental Psychic Pan-gnostic Existence	Serenity Holiness Realization Multiplicity Transparency Righteousness Intuition Inherency
	cardinal Psychic Pan-gnostic Existence	Communion Compassion Knowledge Meaning
	fundamental Psychic Pan-gnostic Existence	Experience Awareness

Subtle Prim-istence	universive Subtle Prim-istence	Pan-gnostic Antistence Pan-gnostic Istence Pan-gnostic Transexistence Pan-gnostic Existence Trans-gnostic Antistence Trans-gnostic Istence Trans-gnostic Transexistence Trans-gnostic Existence
	supreme Subtle Prim-istence	Antistence Nonbeing Istence Nonbeing Transexistence Being Existence Being
	absolute Subtle Holistent Prim-istence	Nonbeing Being

| Causal Holistence | primordial Causal Arch-istent Holistence | Causal Arch-istence
Causal Antiarch-istence ——— |
| | primordial Causal Omni-istent Holistence | Causal Omni-istence
Causal Transomni-istence ——— |

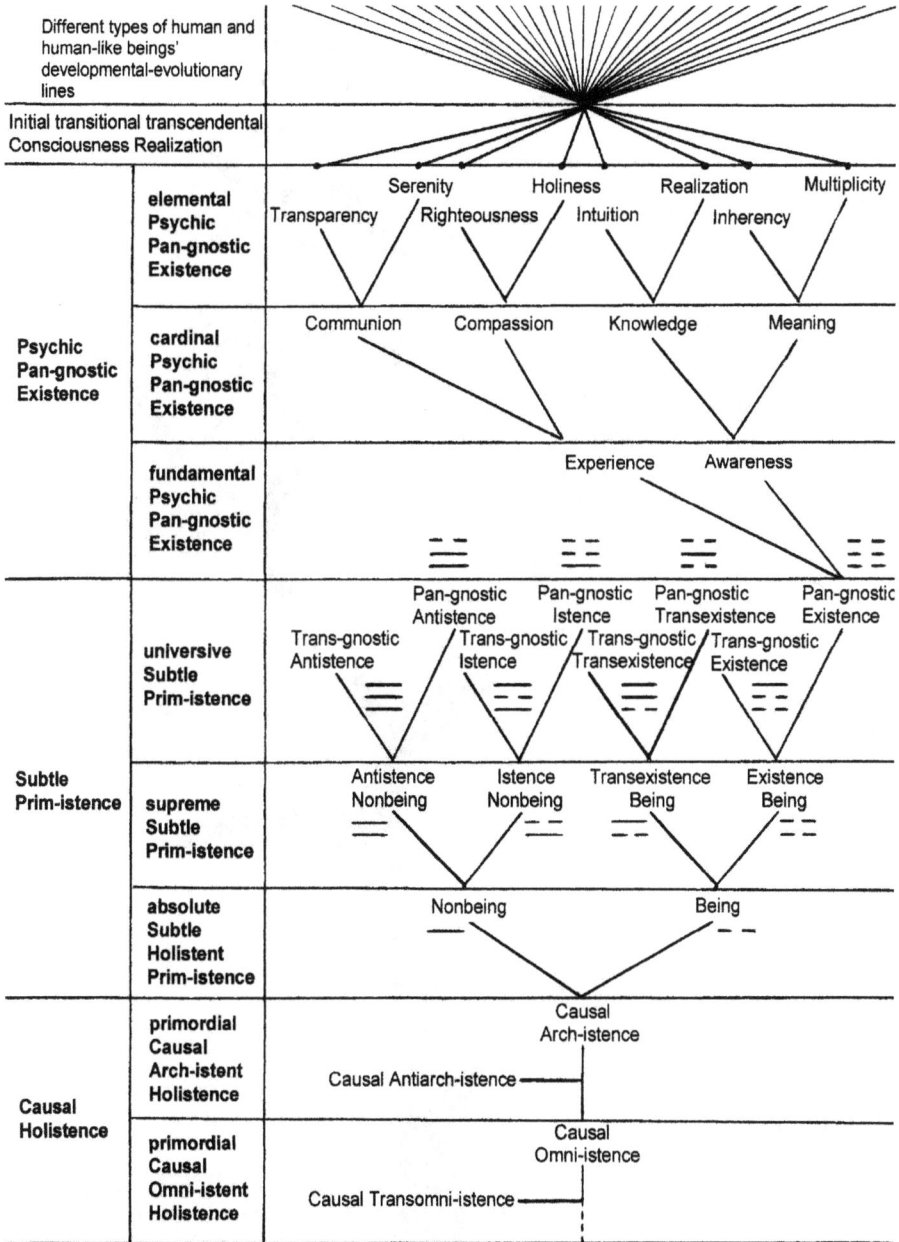

Nondual Spirit-as-Spirit Consciousness Realization

FIGURE 6

44

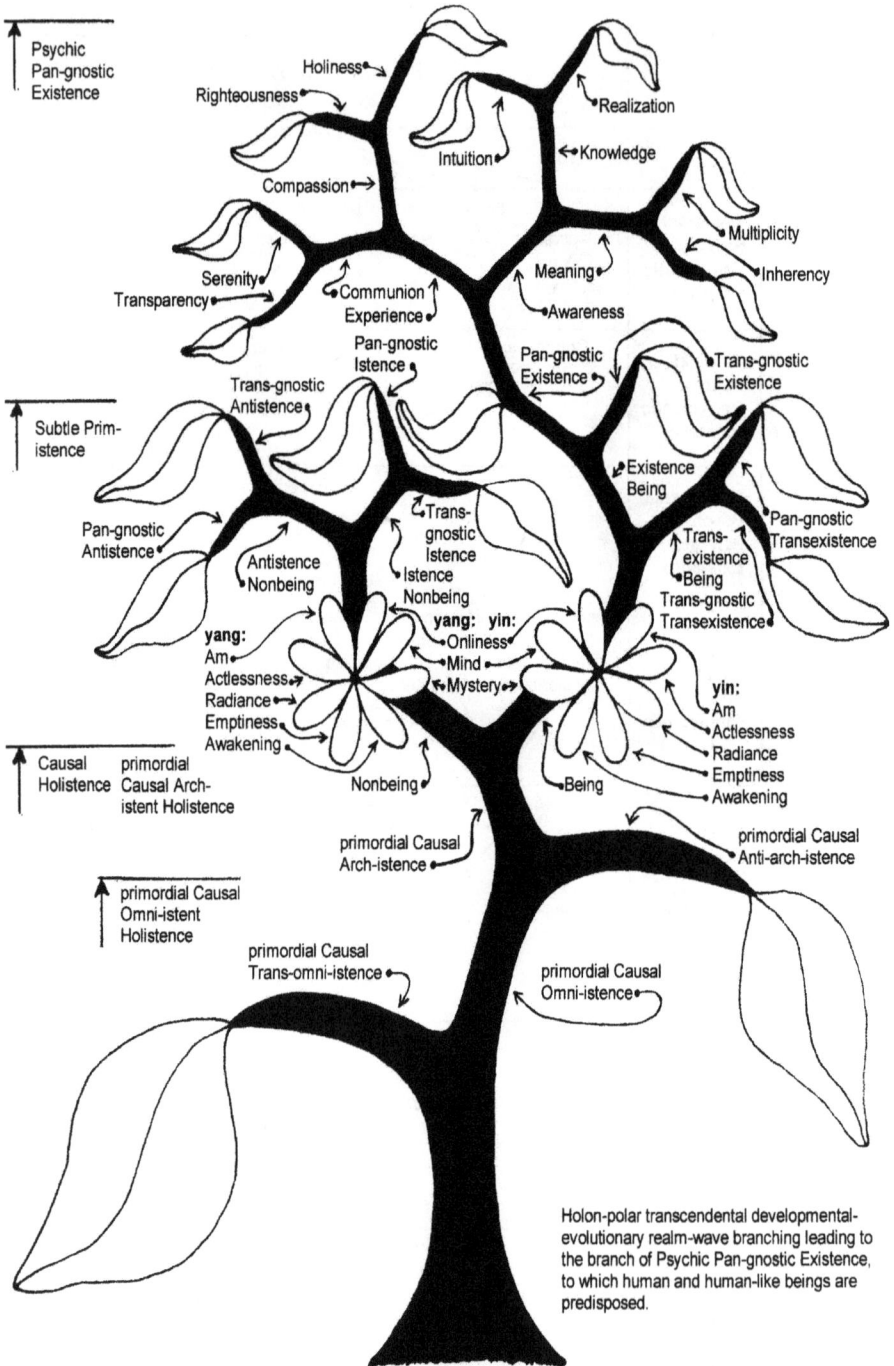

Holon-polar transcendental developmental-
evolutionary realm-wave branching leading to
the branch of Psychic Pan-gnostic Existence,
to which human and human-like beings are
predisposed.

FIGURE 7

VS: This is kind of intricate and difficult to follow. Let me study your diagrams and think about it more. But at this early point in myown development, how do I partake in and embrace the other seven yin-yang Modes of Enlightenment, beyond my native yin-yang Onliness predisposition? (see Figure 5)?

Sage: In Onliness perspective, each Consciousness Being or Entity always has *some* variable degree of predisposition toward, and partakes in, each of the other seven Modes of Awakening in the developmental-evolutionary Ascent-Descent of Self (pointing to Figure 5). Ultimately, as I suggested, when one is developmentally at the transitional termination within *absolute* Subtle Holistent Prim-istence Consciousness (pointing to Figures 4, 6 and 7), all Beings are then *equally* predisposed to, and thus equally partake in, *each* of the eight Enlightenment Modes. And finally, as *pure Witness* within the formless, boundless and unmanifest *Spirit*-Consciousness Realization of *Causal Holistence* Consciousness, all eight Modes are transcended but included, are resolved and integrated, and no longer separately arise or occur in Consciousness (Figures 3, 4, 6 and 7).

VS: But where exactly does earth-centered human development and evolution fit into *this* diagram (pointing to Figure 4)?

Sage: Human Beings' initial *transcendental* development-evolution is symbolized starting at the upper far right of this schematic diagram (pointing to Figure 4), within their *native* predominantly predisposed *diverse being* realm-wave of Pan-gnostic Existence Consciousness. That is, in Onliness theory, human Beings, because of their particular temperament, experiences, configuration, background, composition and structure, are initially predominantly predisposed in their development-evolution to a kind or type of transcendent Consciousness called Pan-gnostic Existence. In this way, among all worlds and universes, Pan-gnostic Existence Consciousness is *one* of the *eight* hypothesized *diverse beings* holon-polar realm-waves of developmental-evolutionary transcendent Consciousness that occur *within* Psychic Multi-istence Consciousness. However, notice in *this* diagram (pointing to Figure 6) that human Beings' developmental-evolutionary course is diagrammed as a separate part of, that is comprises a portion of, this broader more encompassing developmental-evolutionary course diagram (pointing to Figure 4). Finally, note that all four of the *diverse beings* developmental-evolutionary course figures on the upper *left* half of this diagram (pointing to Figure 4) derive from, in the direction of the Descent of Spirit, and evolve, in the direction of the Ascent of Spirit, toward the *unmanifest*, changeless and formless abundant Freedom of *Emptiness* Consciousness, which is identified as Nonbeing Consciousness in Onliness. Conversely, all four *diverse beings* developmental-evolutionary course figures on the upper *right* half of this diagram (Figure 4) derive from and evolve toward the *manifest*, ever-evolving and configurative abundant Fullness of *Form* Consciousness, which is identified as Being Consciousness in Onliness. Note that human Beings' Pan-gnostic Existence based developmental-evolutionary course of Consciousness is predisposed to, derives from and evolves toward, this open and abundant Fullness of *manifest* Being's Consciousness of *Form* (pointing to Figure 4).

VS: This is a lot to take in, and its kind of complex and jargon-loaded for me.

Sage: I'm sorry I can't communicate this more simply and clearly to you. You're right, I do tend to over explain and complexify things.

VS: Yes you do. You have a gift for being obscure and difficult to understand. But are these three realm-waves of Psychic Multi-istence, Subtle Prim-istence and Causal Holistence (pointing to Figure 4) the complete and total number of developmental-evolutionary stages and states of *transcendent* Consciousness for human beings?

Sage: Yes, from the point of view of Onliness, and as seen from high vision-logic realm-wave consciousness. But there's nothing magical about the *number* of holon-polar realm-wave levels or stages and states that are designated. Any number of divisions of transcendental realm-wave stages and states, or Modes of Enlightenment, or diverse beings categories for that matter, could correctly and accurately be designed and designated. Also of course, there are many pre-transcendental holon-polar realm-waves of developmental-evolutionary consciousness *below* transpersonal transcendental Consciousness.

VS: I understand. Could you be an effective spiritual teacher and guide for someone who is not predominantly predisposed to the Onliness Way of Enlightenment Realization?

Sage: Yes. It would take a little more effort and persistence, but it's certainly very possible. Remember that each Consciousness Being or Entity inherently responds to and to some degree functions at *all eight* of the Consciousness Awakening Modes of Enlightenment of Am, Actlessness, Radiance, Emptiness, Awakening, Mystery, Mind, and Onliness (see Figure 5); even as each Being tends to be *predominantly* predisposed to one or the other of these eight Paths.

VS: This is all very abstract stuff. It's far removed from my personal life of regrets, hopes, fears, anger, resentments, frustrations and confusion. What you're telling me doesn't really help me understand or deal with any of these problems, feelings and concerns.

Sage: You're right. You need to focus and work on your particular problems and concerns within your day to day integral transcendental spiritual practice. Within this practice, work on pre-personal, personal and transpersonal issues and realm-wave levels and states of Consciousness; work on interior-subjective and exterior-objective realities, on individual and social-cultural levels; on body, emotion, mind, Soul and Spirit. But don't expect quick fixes or easy answers and solutions.

VS: All of this is discouraging, and seems hopeless to me at times. Its *too* much. It overwhelms me. There are so many and such vast changes I'll need to make in my life.

Sage: These changes will occur on their own, of their own accord, without you having to willfully or forcefully make them. They'll occur as you continue to be committed to and pursue, and in this way deepen and broaden, your transcendental spiritual integral practice. These issues will transform toward resolution as your Consciousness transforms. *If* and *when* such Transformation occurs.

VS: What possible *reason* do I have for doing this work in the first place?

Sage: No reason. The *essence* of what we speak of here is beyond reason; is trans-rational, trans-mental.

VS: That's a hell of a note. Without some reason and logic for the extreme effort and struggle involved in such a transformation of self, *none* of this makes sense.

Sage: As important as reason and logic are in ego self-sense consciousness, and they *are,* Nondual Self-as-Self Consciousness Realization is essentially trans-rational and trans-mental, and completely transcends but includes, negates and preserves, ego-self's reason and logic consciousness.

VS: Then *who* am I doing this for?

Sage: No one and everyone. Vagabond Scholar, You are *Each* and *Every* and *All*; You already *are* the World. There is none other than the Self You always already are. In and through your integral transcendental spiritual practice, You simply have the *opportunity* to Awaken to this Self that is beyond time; uncreated, unconditioned, uncontracted and unknowable.

VS: You're a bit "nutty", do you know that?

Sage: Yes.

VS: You're very grandiose in expression. I don't *feel* anything like the things you think I am. I see myself and the world in very different terms from the way that you describe it. In much more mundane, and even ominous, destructive and dangerous terms. But also at times in constructive, good, compassionate and joyous terms as well. I've never encountered in *this* world the transcendent Self you speak of. Isn't this transcendent Self really just a "wishful thinking" fantasy of yours?

Sage: No. The Consciousness of Self-as-Self is the Reality of *all* realities. And this Nondual Self of Bliss and Freedom is Your *true* and *all-encompassing* Nature and Condition. Vagabond Scholar, You are this Ascending-Descending Alpha and Omega Self of Mystery.

VS: I don't know what to say. You and your words touch me, hold me spellbound in a way, but I fear and doubt them also. I distrust the things you tell me, but still hope that they might *somehow* be somewhat true. What you say confounds me, and that leads me to be suspicious of you, *and* your words.

Sage: Based on your own deepest Awareness and Experience, You must decide *for Yourself* as to the truth or falseness of the things I say.

VS: You're right. For now, I want to pursue and develop my transcendental spiritual integral practice to see where, if anywhere, it may lead me in my life. But I feel alone and "out on a limb" with this decision, and its direction too. Isolated, except for the support you offer me.

Sage: Seek out others, perhaps a group of others, who pursue a spiritual practice similar to your own, and share that practice with them. They can offer you important information, ideas and support.

VS: That's a good idea. I'll check into this possibility. But coming back to the idea of a *transcendent* Self, I'm wondering if your Onliness perspective of Self, of Spirit, is perhaps just a means that you use, consciously or unconsciously, in an attempt to deny the reality of your own mortality and inevitable death?

Sage: No. In manifest Reality, as the Buddha indicates, *all* phenomena are impermanent. All things of manifest Reality arise and pass. Beings are born and beings die, but in the Eyes of timeless Self this has no *special* meaning or importance. It's essentially inconsequential. The Self that You are, this Consciousness of All and None, is neither born nor does it die. And, transcending time and space, *unqualifiable Self* is each and every Being's only and true Identity, Nature and Condition.

VS: What you say about death and dying may be abstractly true, but it's also very cold and chevalier. When a loved one dies there's much personal and very real suffering, anguish, sorrow and sadness. And often great joy and happiness with the birth of a new child into one's family.

Sage: Of course, that is true. I don't mean in any way to dismiss or discount the real *personal* suffering, despair and pain that accompanies the death of a loved one, which occurs at this personal egoic level of consciousness. Or the great personal joy and happiness that can accompany the birth of a new child.

VS: From your perspective then, is the death of a human being, or any being for that matter, the end or death of *all* their consciousness? Is there anything about that human that lives on or exists after their death?

Sage: "Lives on" and "exists" implies a time dimension. Self is prior to and thus transcends but includes time, as I've said. Nondual transcendent Consciousness of Self-as-Self, of Spirit-as-Spirit, neither lives nor dies in time and space, but rather negates and preserves both life and death in space-time. Thus, this boundless and timeless Consciousness that *You* truly are does not die, and cannot die, with the manifest bodymind's temporal death.

VS: But, beyond others' memories of me, will anything about me as a person, about myself and my personal life, my ideas and relationships, live on and survive my death?

Sage: In my view, *no*; not in the personal-egoic temporal consciousness sense that you imply. However, this bodymind egoic and pre-egoic consciousness as a manifest expression of Self is certainly always present as Self, included but transcended; and thus is not in this *trans-egoic* sense "lost" or "forgotten" or "discarded".

VS: After death, can I then at all continue to recall and evoke the life of my egoic self as a person in the world?

Sage: I suspect not. Unborn and undying, Self-as-Self includes and embraces *all* of manifest Form and unmanifest Emptiness, and You are *This* and This only. Thus, birth and death in time and space do not and cannot arise for Self, for Spirit-as-Spirit. But, in my opinion, with the temporal death of your bodymind personal self, all temporal personal-egoic and pre-egoic consciousness ends, and no longer arises or returns. Nondual Self-as-Self's transcendent Wisdom and Truth, and immanent Compassion and Care thus *transcend* but include this temporal death of personal bodymind consciousness.

VS: I think I understand what you're saying, but it's confusing too. You often seem to go out of your way to confuse and confound me. At the same time, I have the gnawing feeling that what you say may at least be partly true. But again, this is all pure speculation on your part. Is it not?

Sage: In relation to pre-egoic, pre-personal and personal egoic consciousness *after* the temporal death of bodymind self, yes it is speculation and opinion.

VS: You often use the terms "holon" and "holonic", and I'm not sure what they mean?

Sage: As Ken Wilber and others before him have said, "holon" and "holonic" are terms that describe the *creative* underlying developmental-evolutionary *structural patterning* of Reality; with the exception, according to Onliness theory, of Nondual

Self-as-Self Consciousness Realization Reality. Holons are repeatedly nested whole/part sequences or levels of increasing complexity and inclusion in developmental-evolutionary Reality. Nested holons are said to emerge in the course of development-evolution's process of creative novelty. A holon is best described as a *whole/part* in that it is *at once* both a new and unique, and more Consciousness inclusive, *whole* level of development-evolution that *transcends* all of its previous junior, less Consciousness inclusive, holon levels that preceded it, or are under it. But it also *includes,* as its *parts,* all of these junior developmental-evolutionary holons in a sequentially nested manner. It thus at once negates and preserves these junior holon levels and states of Reality or Consciousness. And in the course of continuing development-evolution, this recently new and unique emergent holon next, itself, becomes a *part* in and of a yet newer and unique emerging *whole*, an even *more* novel and Consciousness inclusive developmental-evolutionary senior holon Reality, that emerges *through,* more than *from,* this now junior holon, and is above it. This newly emerging senior holon thus, in turn, transcends but includes as a part, the now junior holon and all the holons below it, in this same nested way. This developmental-evolutionary progressive and creative novelty of *nested* whole/part holonic structural patterning is said to extend in Reality "all the way up and all the way down". (Sage takes Figure 2 from her pocket, unfolds it and shows it to VS) This is a visual diagrammatic example of this structural holonic nesting patterning and sequence.

VS: I understand, but this is a very generalized and abstract way to describe the developmental-evolutionary structural pattern of reality, is it not?

Sage: You're right, it's very abstract and non-specific, but insightful, useful and revealing also.

VS: But when you speak of holons you always associate and somehow link them with polarity and polarity-within-unity ideas. Why do you do this?

Sage: The patterning of polarity-within-unity is of *central* importance in Onliness conception. Onliness theory asserts that, like holons and holonic patterning, polarity-with-unity, that is polaric patterning, is an *inherent* structural dimension and feature of all of *manifest* Reality, and thus of each expression of manifest Form Consciousness. Onliness claims that polarity-within-unity is a *deep* and *fundamental* aspect of both pre-transcendental and transcendental manifest Consciousness *up to*, and the shadow of it slightly into, transcendent *unmanifest, boundless* and *formless* Causal Holistence Consciousness; at which developmental-evolutionary point polarity-within-unity is dissipated and deconstructed, is transcended but included, and no longer inherently arises and occurs in Consciousness. In Onliness perspective, holonic structural patterning alone, so called holon-only patterning, developmentally-evolutionarily continues throughout unmanifest, boundless and formless Causal Holistence Consciousness. But then holonic-only patterning also dissipates and deconstructs, is transcended but included, and no longer inherently arises or occurs with the completion of Causal Holistence realm-wave Consciousness; and thus does not at all arise or occur in the subsequent Realization of Nondual Self-as-Self Consciousness Enlightenment. Recall that Onliness theory asserts that Self of Nondual Consciousness Awakening is *trans-holonic* in the sense that although such Enlightenment includes but transcends all junior holons below It and is a new, original and unique Realization *whole* Itself, this Self of Absolute Reality is *never*, in turn, Absolutely transcended and included; is never superseded and replaced by a subsequent holon above It. Which is to say that such Enlightenment is Absolute, like the Reality It Is. In this way, as I've said, Nondual Self of Absolute Reality Consciousness is neither holonic nor is it not holonic, and *both*.

VS: This is kind of complex and complicated. What then is the connection or relationship *between* holonic and polaric patterning in Onliness theory?

Sage: (Sage removes and unfolds Figure 1 from her pocket and spreads it out between them) This is a schematic diagram example of the *integrated* patterning relationship between holonic and polaric interaction. The *three nested sets* of two touching circles each are the three holons. Each of the *two* touching circles themselves, of these three circle sets, are the *two* poles of the polarity-within-unity of and within each of these three nested holon (Sage point to each of these imaged patterns as she speaks). Onliness theory claims that this polaric structural patterning, of polarity-with-unity, is an *innate* and *integral* feature of holonic process itself. That is, that such polaric patterning is an *inherent dimension* of holonic manifest Consciousness, up to the developmental-evolutionary emergence of Causal Holistence realm-wave Consciousness.

VS: All the things you've told me, your ideas, are somewhat interesting, but are presented in a very scholarly stiff and bookish way; in a kind of professorial and somewhat boring manner. You seem to keep yourself at a safe and impersonal emotional distance from me. And even though we've spoken several times, I really don't know you up close and personal. I don't get a clear sense of who you are as a *person*.

Sage: I'm sorry to hear that, and sorry you feel this way. Within personal-ego consciousness, it's true, I *am* a scholarly and bookish person. I'm not an unusual person, and certainly not an especially exciting or charismatic person; or particularly striking in appearance. I've already mentioned some of the problematic personality-trait tendencies I have, so you know of me in that way. I tend to be a very common and down-to-earth *functionally* oriented person, who sees and enjoys humor in the antics and folly of my own actions and life; as well as in the antics and folly of humanity in general. But also I'm aware of the sadness, pain, anguish, suffering and struggle in this world. In any case, it's not necessary that you know me personally for me to be an effective teacher and guide for you, if teacher and guide is what you want.

VS: I guess I just wonder about you; what you're like and who you are. And what *is* this Self you claim to be, and that you say I always already am.

Sage: That's certainly understandable. (Sage pauses briefly) As I've indicated, Nondual Consciousness Self-as-Self Remembrance and Realization transcends but includes both holonic and polaric, that is polarity-within-unity, Realities. This *unfathomable* Self of no-self that each and every Being completely and only is, which ultimately is trans-holonic and trans-polaric, is the transcendent Ground, Goal and Source *of* and *from* which all Consciousness realm-waves arise, and to which they all return. Nondual Self-as-Self is trans-polaric in that subject-object polarity-duality Consciousness no longer arises or occurs in Consciousness. Witness-and-that-which-is-witnessed are no longer two, nor not-two.

VS: That's hard to understand. How does Nondual Consciousness Self Realization transcend subject-object polarity-duality?

Sage: Nondual Self-as-Self Consciousness has no second or opposite. There is no outside-ness or beyond-ness *to* It, or *of* It. There is no *otherness* to Spirit-as-Spirit Awakening, and thus no polaric or dualistic subject-object distinction or *separateness*.

VS: As Nondual Realization Self of Consciousness then, I am the *other* as much as, and the same as, I am *myself*. There's no division or separation between us, is that right?

Sage: That's right. You are, right now, No-separation, Oneness Self of Onliness. You are Complete and Seamless Self of Radiance. In This, there is no otherness or boundary *whatsoever* between I and Thou.

VS: Dream on, Sage. Dream on.

The scene slowly darkens and fades from view into blackness.

Act 2, Scene 1

Sage and Vagabond Scholar sit alone on the grass and dry clay ground next to and partially facing one another before a small campfire with a metal cooking grate over it. It is a warm summer day in late afternoon and the sun is close to setting, but still brightly lit and glowing in blue skies. These two are in the western North Dakota Badlands, seated in view of the Little Missouri River, two hundred yards or so behind them. Beyond the river are the high and rugged multi-colored badland buttes, lit by the nearly setting sunlight. The faint sounds of birds and the soft sound of the flowing river can be heard. The scent of sage is in the air. The two figures are heating canned beans in a small pan on the fire's grate. Later, the beans are poured onto paper plates, and with their spoons the two eat these as they talk. Along with this, each eats a sandwich and an apple, and drinks water from their shared canteen.

Sage: There are severe limits as to what I can tell you in words, even from a high vision-logic realm-wave level and state of consciousness. There's much that cannot be Understood and Realized from even this advanced ego consciousness perspective.

VS: What kinds of limits do you mean?

Sage: The wellspring-source of language is integrally founded and based upon polarity-within-unity. And because of the inherent dualistic nature of such polarity in language, the final meanings and implications that language can convey, when such meanings are pursued to their deepest source, are ultimately and profoundly paradoxical and self-contradictory. In this way, words can never convey the *direct* Realization of Truth, of Realty Itself. As a teacher, this can most often be better accomplished through example, or by pointing, or merely silence. My Zen Buddhist teacher Nonin Chowaney-roshi has written "I've learned from my teachers by closely observing how they live. I never heard Ikko Narasaki say a harsh word about anyone when I was studying with him in Japan, and when I put down other people, he responded with silence. This silence struck with great force and taught me more about following the practice of right speech and the precept of not extolling the self by putting down others than any of his dharma talks on these subjects."

VS: But how should I go about my *own* journey of understanding Reality or Truth?

Sage: Through your continuing body, mind, Soul and Spirit interior-subjective and exterior-objective, individual and communal, *all-levels, all quadrants* integral transcendental spiritual practice. Through this, You can directly Experience and Realize Reality for Yourself. But *also,* other people, through their words, pointing, example, and silence, can advise, encourage and help You on this Journey.

VS: It's been about a year since I last spoke with you. I've continued my practice over this time as you've directed, and its been helpful I think. I've calmed down a bit and am able to see myself, my life, in broader and more generous terms. I do experience strange states of consciousness at times in zazen meditation, that's for sure. I don't really know what to make of them, if anything. They are sometimes serene, without content and empty, but kind of unnerving and in a way disturbing too. But mostly my mind wanders to past or upcoming everyday events and concerns, from one thing to another.

Sage: Keep up and intensify your integral transcendental spiritual practice. When mind wander in meditation, return focus of attention to breath only. You're doing fine.

VS: I'm starting to see my life differently, in a new way. From within a somewhat different and kinder frame of reference. And with this, I see others differently too. I see their struggles and efforts, and have more compassion toward them. They seem closer to me, and I feel and have more patience and loving kindness toward them. What do you make of this?

Sage: Your transcendent Heart-Self is beginning to open up, both to Yourself and to other Beings also. You're starting to Remember *who* You are: this Infinite Uncontracted Self of Am. This is a *glimmer* and *glimpse* of Recognition and Awakening into Your own True Nature and Condition.

VS: Maybe so, but almost all of my life is still personal-ego oriented and driven; about me and my and mine. A kind of "what's in it for me" mentality. This Awakening to Inherent, Illuminated Self that you've invited and encouraged me to take, and that I've taken, is a very slow endeavor and difficult ordeal. Am I just wasting the moments of my life in this way?

Sage: No. In life, every moment here is profound and important. Even those moments that ego-self judges to be the most painful and difficult, or boring and mundane. Full transcendent Recognition and Realization of Self-as-Self is present here in *each* and *every* moment. Do not be deluded by ego's sense of separate-self perceptions and mentality; ego's sense of isolation and separateness.

VS: At times, I get down-hearted and depressed with my life in this practice. I start to think, what's the *use* of it, what possible difference does it make; what *purpose* does it have at all?

Sage: Don't doubt Your integral transcendental spiritual practice's usefulness. In a relative sense, it has the highest purpose and makes the greatest difference. It is the difference between the *personal* self's egoic consciousness of narcissistic ignorance and delusion, and the transcendental Consciousness Awakening to Reality, to Truth, to *transpersonal* Self-as-Self. What is it that could possibly be *more* important than the Self's Enlightenment of Wisdom and Compassion?

VS: I understand. But within the life of personal egoic self there's so much fear, sorrow and suffering; and in the world at large such great privation, violence, cruelty, suffering and indifference. It seems overwhelming and hopeless at times. These are concerns and problems that *cry out* for practical and concrete action and solutions *here* and *now*, and not through some esoteric and impractical individual spiritual practices that *may* come to fruition at some distant future time.

Sage: A person's *integral* transcendental spiritual practice, which includes interior-subjective and exterior-objective, individual and communal, work on body, emotion, mind, Soul, and Spirit can, *right* here and now, and in very specific and practical ways, address all of the real and profound problems and concerns that you describe.

VS: The actions and solutions *you* put forward to these pressing and often horrific personal and societal problems are very *vague* and *general*. Be more specific. For example, what am I to do in the face of immanent and life threatening violence and aggression by someone toward me, or toward a loved one?

Sage: I can only speak to you of this in terms of my personal ego-individual *mental* ideas and opinions, which are strongly determined by my particular personal, social, cultural, and historical contextual background and conditions. These opinions then are not of trans-mental, transpersonal Knowledge or Understanding. Given the situation and circumstance you describe, first use your egoic planning skills and means to avoid such violence and aggression toward you or others. If that's not possible or ultimately fails, and no other options of avoidance or escape present themselves, then use a minimum of violence and aggression to *disable* the aggressor, and thus defend yourself or your loved one. And in this dire situation it is critically important that you *do* defend and protect yourself and loved one. Above *all* however, avoid violent action that may result in the death of, or serious injury to, the aggressor. As a *last* resort in such an extreme circumstance then, you need to act to quickly and completely disable the aggressor by *any* means available to you, but without serious injury to or killing of such a person. And when disabled, immediately attempt to care for and preserve the life of the aggressor, if need be. But more broadly speaking, *do not* under any circumstances, directly or indirectly, participate or become involved in wars or mass-societal violence and conflicts of any sort, for any reason. Involvement or participation in such aggression, violence and murder is completely morally obscene and unacceptable. Mass-societal conflicts must be resolved, no matter how long it takes, through various and diverse non-violent means.

VS: Let's say the best preventative efforts have failed, and the leaders of one localized nation or regional state are capable of and *determined* to violently attack and destroy the leaders and people of another nation or regional state. Given you proposed conditions, how can this be prevented or stopped?

Sage: First of all, work early on toward the establishment of a democratically elected strong and integrated cooperative world community government, and thus the elimination of the so called sovereign nation-states and their repeated tendency to war with on another. But more immediate to your question, if *all* individuals refuse to directly or indirectly participate in, or in any way support, wars or mass-societal conflicts, refuse to devise and create weapons, armies and so on, then the situation you describe would not arise to begin with. But again, to deal with such conflict there needs to exist a strong and democratically elected world community governing body that has full legal authority, power, will and means to effectively and assertively intervene in a variety of both positive and punitive ways in the kinds of conflict you describe, but *without* the serious injury to or killing of people. And in this way, it must be able to aggressively and promptly prevent and arrest such attempted geographically localized violent attacks by one region on its neighboring regional areas. In the instance of such world governing body intervention however, aggressive violent action, *not* including the murder or serious injury of people, would be the *last* option and resort, after all other options have failed.

VS: That all sounds very righteous and morally correct, but that's not how the world works. That's *not* the way most people function in this world. To me, it sounds like you're living in a dream. Very often, and probably for the most part, people are covetous, greedy, aggressive, clannish and violent, and don't give a damn about high-minded platitudes on righteousness, non-violence and morality. To most people, ideas like yours are just a joke, or at best a pie-in-the-sky dream.

Sage: What you say is, I think, an accurate *partial truth* about the personal consciousness status and condition of many, if not most, human beings at the present time.

VS: But beyond human to human interaction, how would you propose humans deal with and relate to other sentient beings; other animals for example?

Sage: I suggest that the human cruelty of confinement and killing of other animals for humans to eat as food creates great suffering for these animals, and is completely unnecessary as a source of human nutrition. You need to *minimize* the intentional injury and killing, and thus suffering, of *all* sentient Beings, including plants and animals; indeed of all Consciousness Entities. Of course, in order to exist in manifest reality, humans and virtually all other beings must and will, inadvertently and sometimes purposefully, injure and kill countless numbers of other organisms, microscopic and macroscopic, in order to survive. For example, this occurs in the process of digestion, in the immune system's fighting off and killing of pathogenic organisms, and so on. And also in other various inadvertent and unintentional ways in which we injure and kill other beings, even when taking the required extra care to avoid doing so.

VS: Then you think we should all be vegetarians?

Sage: Being a vegetarian is one important way to minimize the suffering of other complex animals who possess, from the point of view of *relative* reality, complex advanced consciousness. But understand that in transcendent *Absolute Reality* of Self or Spirit, *all* manifest Consciousness Expressions or Entities are, each and every Entity is, of the same and equal Buddha-mind and Buddha-nature; all are of one and the same, and equal, in transcendental Consciousness and Importance, without distinction or discrimination.

VS: Once again, for at least half of the human population of this world, you've managed to put a stick into and stir up a hornet's nest. Nice going. Fortunately I'm already a vegetarian for the most part, and have been for many years. However, I do each fish and seafood from time to time. Are you a vegetarian?

Sage: Yes.

VS: To come back to Enlightenment Realization, you, and others too, have suggested that to transcendentally Awaken, to Realize Enlightenment, one must *sequentially* develop through, and indeed in general beings must sequentially evolve *to*, various progressively more consciousness-inclusive realm-wave stages and states of consciousness, including several stages and states of transcendental Consciousness. Is that correct?

Sage: Yes. In Onliness perspective (see Figures 3, 4, 5, 6 and 7), as I explained to you, there are three such successive co-created worldspace realm-waves of transcendent developmental-evolutionary Consciousness. In succession, I call these realm-waves Psychic Multi-istence, followed by Subtle Prim-istence, followed by Causal Holistence. Developmentally-evolutionarily, after Causal Holistence Consciousness Realization there can arise and emerge the transcendence and inclusion of all worldspaces, the "Worldspace" of all worldspaces so to speak, called Nondual Spirit-as-Spirit or Self-as-Self Consciousness Awakening. This unborn and undying *Am* of always already Buddha-mind Enlightenment. This Luminous Self of *selfless* Godhead, Atman-Brahman, Christ-consciousness, Buddha-nature.

VS: But must I develop in sequence through each of these Consciousness realm-waves in this order of succession before the possible developmental emergence of such Enlightenment?

Sage: Yes; in *this* order without exception and *without* realm-wave stage omission; or by whatever other numbers of similar realm-wave stages and states that these three may be divided into; or by whatever other names these realm-waves may be called.

VS: You kind of enjoy making this as difficult as possible, don't you. How long then will it take me to develop in this way, so as to Realize Nondual Spirit-as-Spirit Consciousness Awakening?

Sage: No one an tell you that. Perhaps a millisecond, perhaps a million lifetimes.

VS: Very helpful.

Sage: Remember, Nondual Self-as-Self Consciousness Realization is not a goal for you to attain or achieve; indeed is not achievable or possessable at all, but rather is ordinary and everyday, is always already Your and My true Nature and Condition - infinitely, eternally, unconditionally.

VS: But I have no *sense* of this, no *feeling* for it. I just can't grasp the way you say I am. I can't comprehend myself in this light, as having access to and actually being such transcendent Kosmocentric Consciousness.

Sage: Vagabond Scholar please understand, You and I, but not merely as our ego-bodymind alone, *already are*, ever have been and will ever be, this *Self* of Enlightened Buddha-nature, Christ-consciousness, God-consciousness, and Atman-Brahman. This Numinous Revelation Self of Am.

VS: Sage, you generously share with me your conceptions and ideas, which are lofty and high-minded if somewhat strange; and you described for me your way of practicing, which I've followed for the most part. I see in all of this some validity and truth, but I'm also by nature cautious and skeptical. I appreciate all you've shared with me, but often it seems so self-centered and self absorbed.

Sage: All that I've told You is toward *ending* and *transcending* personal self absorption and self-centeredness. Toward Recognizing the profound importance of We, and Us, and Thou; the great significance of gratitude for and appreciation of other sentient Beings. The *centrality* of transcendent Compassion and Loving Kindness toward Others is in all I've said to You. And the importance of developmentally realizing a strong, integrated and mature *ethical* and *moral* personal ego-self, as a structural support and dimension of such Compassion, is central in all I've said to You.

VS: Yes, you're right, Compassion for others has been prominent in the thoughts you've shared with me.

Sage: I also need to better emphasize to You the importance of living a simple, modest, humble and peaceful life with others in this everyday world of birth and death. And also the importance of *silence* and *solitude* in Your life and practice. And finally, the importance of bowing in your daily meditation practice, as a gesture of gratitude to and appreciation for other Beings. Remember to reverently and repeatedly bow in the course of Your daily meditation practice, as I've shown you, in acknowledgement of, appreciation for, and gratitude to *Everyone* and *Everything*. And thus as a gesture of gratitude, appreciation and acknowledgement to the Divine Self-as-Self You are, which *all-inclusively* embraces the Many and the One, manifest Form and unmanifest Emptiness, Nirvana and Samsara.

VS: I understand. Sage, how does Nondual Self-as-Self Realization Consciousness *see* or *perceive,* and thus *experience,* Reality Itself?

Sage: In personal ego consciousness you see reality from only *one* perspective at a time. Self-as-Self Nondual Consciousness, which You truly are, does not *view* Reality as object, but rather *is* Reality Itself; *Is* Truth Itself without a second or opposite. And Self *Sees* the Reality It *Is* not only from *one* perspective, but rather from *each* and *all* perspectives *at once*. In this way, Self-as-Self Realization Consciousness *is* Reality and *Sees* Reality just as It truly Is; *simultaneously* from *all* perspectives. Self of Nondual Realization Consciousness is both the *Seer* and the *Seen* because subject-object duality consciousness is *transcended* but included, and thus no longer arises or occurs.

VS: Again, this is very esoteric. Aren't you and I, in our obsessive preoccupation with Enlightenment, living in a kind of isolated and protected ivy tower? While so many, if not most, of the world's human beings are suffering in very difficult or even desperate situations of various combinations of hunger, lack of even minimally adequate shelter, endlessly long hours of boring and difficult labor, sickness, pain and disease, wars, horrific and chronic exploitations, and often abuse, we sit here in our secure cocoon contemplating our navels.

Sage: (smiles and softly laughs) We must of course *always* be mindful of the often severe and even overwhelming burdens, pain and suffering that all earthly humans, and indeed all Beings, experience and endure. And it is our ongoing daily *integral* transcendental spiritual practice that can facilitate the lessening of such burdens, pain and suffering for Others. Indeed, as Self, we *are* these, quote-unquote, "others"; We *are* this very World. In Truth, the developmental-evolutionary Awakening to Self-as-Self is the *central key* to ending suffering, and is thus of urgent and critical importance to each and every Being.

VS: But the individual *ordeal* and *process* of Enlightenment seems so laborious, gradual and indirect in this regard. It's like the water of care and compassion slowly dripping from a faucet in an vain attempt to displace a giant ocean of privation, pain and suffering.

Sage: What authentic and thorough, comprehensive and enduring, alternative would you suggest?

VS: I don't know. But if and when, in the course of human evolution and development, there can progressively emerge greater

Wisdom and Compassion in many Beings of Consciousness, toward Enlightenment as you suggest, will there not then gradually occur progressively more compassionate and caring individual and communal solutions, that is to say more just, equitable, effective and humane solutions, to *all* of these human problems?

Sage: Yes, I think so; *if* and *when* such development and evolution occurs. But such progressive earth-centered human development-evolution toward and of transcendent Wisdom and Compassion is *not* pre-designed, pre-destined, pre-ordained or pre-determined by any means.

The scene slowly darkens and fades from view into blackness.

Act 2, Scene 2

Sage and Vagabond Scholar are seated in camping chairs on a rocky ledge at the edge of and overlooking the amazing vista of Arizona's Grand Canyon. They are seated partially facing the audience, with a nearly full and breathtaking view of the Grand Canyon in both their own and the audience's view. They sit in the shade of a Juniper tree on a warm and mostly sunny early afternoon, with billowing white clouds floating high above. The scent of sage and quiet songs of birds are in the air. The two are alone in a secluded area along the Canyon's rim. As they talk they share a can of peanuts and a canteen of water, which each samples from time to time.

VS: In Onliness, what exactly do you mean by the transcendent Ascent and immanent Descent of Spirit or Self?

Sage: Structurally, there are three foundational pillars upon which the evolution and development of Onliness Way of Enlightenment is established. These are transcendent Wisdom, Compassion and Communion. In Onliness, Wisdom is a function of transcendent Knowledge and Meaning (see Figures 5, 6 and 7). But *functionally*, one can say that Onliness, like all of the seven other Modes of Enlightenment, walks on the two legs of transcendent Wisdom and immanent Compassion, since Communion is implied and inherent in both. Onliness suggests that, to *widely varying* degrees, each Being at each and every sub-transcendental and transcendental evolutionary-developmental level and state of Spirit's Consciousness, *concurrently* embraces and expresses *both* the transcendent Ascent of Wisdom and Insight, that is Eros, toward Nondual Consciousness Realization, *as well as* the immanent Descent of Compassion and Care, which is Agape, toward each and every Consciousness Being and Entity.

VS: But *specifically* how, and in what way, is this immanent Descent of Compassion and Care embraced and expressed?

Sage: In an endless multitude of ways, great and small, in relation to self and others over the course of our ordinary day to day lives and activities. You *See* the manifest expressions and results of selfishness, sickness, pain, privation, cruelty, exploitation, greed, indifference, violence, and even rape, killing and murder, around you in the world. You *Know* what needs to be done, and what *You* need to do to reduce and eliminate the suffering and injustice that these cause. Just *do* it, and keep doing it. In broad terms, such Compassion and Care finds expression through our profound concern and attention to, and sustained concerted efforts toward, the *hard work* of reducing and eliminating the privation, exploitation, sickness, pain and suffering of all Beings and Entities, whenever, however and wherever this suffering and injustice occurs.

VS: That's a tall order. And it sounds kind of *unrealistic*, given certain, and not infrequent, greedy, indifferent and violent human inclinations and proclivities. The human problems underlying all of this seem *so* overwhelming and pervasive.

Sage: But you can step forward in each moment and *do* what you *can* do, day to day. With gratitude, and in the application of Loving Kindness, appreciate and enjoy your embodiment as a human within this beautiful, but often troubled, earth-centered existence. Such human embodiment is a *profound* and *wondrous* gift and opportunity.

VS: My earth-centered human existence seldom feels at all profound or wondrous to me. More often than not it feels drab, tiresome, frustrating, irritating, angering and exhausting. And only very rarely exhilarating, exciting, beautiful and serene. Do you get angry and frustrated at times?

Sage: Of course. I experience *all* of the emotions you just mentioned. But I don't identify myself *as* these emotions and thus get lost, engulfed and embedded in them. I try not to be consumed by or drown in these emotions, positive or negative, but rather let them arise and pass; and in this way let go of them. Instead of clinging to them then, I try to Witness such emotions as the passing pre-personal and personal-egoic consciousness manifestations that in Reality they are. Thus they tend to be fleeting and pass from Consciousness quite rapidly.

VS: Then one has to *continue* to work on developmental problems and issues of pre-egoic and pre-personal as well as personal-egoic consciousness, even in advanced realm-wave stages and states of transcendent Consciousness Awakening, in which you are; perhaps even in Nondual Self-as-Self Realization Consciousness. Is that right?

Sage: Yes. From Onliness perspective, even manifest Beings who Realize Self of Nondual Consciousness Awakening will still need to continue to work, within the Fullness of manifest Form, on pre-personal and personal shadow problematic developmental areas, but in Ways that *transcend* but include the ways of not yet Awakened manifest Beings. That is to say, for example, in the way of Witnessing of emotions that I've just described. But you're correct, Beings within *all* manifest Form Realities of holonic-polaric and holon-only Consciousness development, and even *beyond* this as Nondual Spirit-as-Spirit Consciousness Realized Beings - and yet *still* manifest Beings, must continue to *integrally* work on all shadow-problematic developmental-evolutionary issues within all worldspace realm-wave levels and states of Consciousness.

VS: So, such an Enlightened Being would have to *continue* to work on any line or realm-wave stage and state of that Being's developmental Consciousness where there remains a delay, problem, barrier, or neurotic shadow pathology of any sort?

Sage: That's right. Problematic issues and even shadow or pathologic consciousness areas for such a Being could include concerns involving development of body, mind, emotions, sexuality, interpersonal relations, social, political, vocational, scientific, artistic, cultural, Soul or Spirit; indeed, *all* problematic lines and realm-wave levels and states that implicate and involve Beauty, Truth and Goodness.

VS: It's been four years since we first met and talked with one another. It's been nearly that long since I've taken up the integral transcendental spiritual practice you adopted from those who formulated and developed it, especially the philosopher Ken Wilber but also with contributions from teachers like Michael Murphy, Andrew Cohen, Terry Patten, Adam Leonard, Mirco Morelli, Craig Hamilton, Jeff Salzman and others too; and then you adapted and applied it for use in the Way of Onlness. Sage, you've been my primary teacher and guide over these four years. In this practice, I've learned a great deal and developed in transcendental Awareness and Experience. I now respond with greater caring and compassion toward other beings than I previously did. Also, I think I have a deeper understanding of and insight into the transcendent spiritual nature of my life, and of the lives of my fellow beings. I thank you for that, and for being my teacher and guide over these years.

Sage: You're welcome. But you've just begun the journey of Awakening to Self, to Spirit, and have *far* to go.

VS: I know. I know. In the sequence of Enlightenment symbolized through the "10 Bulls of Zen" described in Paul Reps' book *Zen Flesh, Zen Bones,* I feel I'm at the third level, which say: "I hear the song of the nightingale. The sun is warm, the wind is mild, willows are green along the shore, Here no bull can hide! What artist can draw that massive head, those majestic horns?"

Sage: I think you're assessment is correct.

VS: But in this journey and ordeal, where do I go from here? *How* do I proceed? What must I *do,* and in what way do I do it?

Sage: A wise Zen Buddhist Master once responded to such a question by simply saying "Walk on." I would say the same. Another sage Zen Master has said "Everyday Mind is the Way". Also good advice I think.

VS: But I'm doubtful, weary and afraid. I feel inadequate to and unprepared for the task just now before me, and for the journey that lies ahead.

Sage: You already *are* that task and that journey. You always are and ever have been that Divine Awakened Self of Consciousness, which is Enlightenment. You are, right now, this *Unqualifiable* Spirit; the infinite and boundless Radiance of Worlds.

VS: That's easy for you to say, but hard for me to accept and comprehend.

(The two sit in silence for a short time.)

VS: Can you clarify for me what exactly you mean when you say that Tao of Onliness theory and perspective is, in a *broadly* defined sense, empirically testable?

Sage: Simply metaphysically *asserting* that a fixed and external transcendental concept, principle or idea *eternally* exists and is *eternally* true, does not cause it to *actually* Exist or mean that in Reality it is True. Onliness theory has the potential of falsifiability in that its practice *applications* and *predicted* practice outcomes are directly experientially testable; and thus it is, in this broadly defined sense, empirically testable. Onliness theory does not metaphysically assert the *necessary truth* of its concepts, principles, ideas and practices, but rather asks you to *apply* these by experientially testing them out for yourself. And in this way to gather the data so as to see if they are either *true,* in the sense that they facilitate, or *false,* in the sense that they do not facilitate, your own spiritual development and growth in relation to Onliness theory predictions. Thus, Onliness theory has falsifiability in that the *applications* of its tenets, hypotheses, conceptions, and practices can be *directly* experientially, that is empirically, tested to determine their truthfulness or falseness in relation to its predictions. The generalize process involved in such experiential assessment is as follows: If you are willing to thoroughly learn and practice the knowledge and skills that are *needed to test* Onliness theory in one or more of its dimensions, it can *then* be tested by *directly* experiencing for yourself, gathering the data, as to whether these dimensions are true or false for you in relation to Onliness theory predicted development toward transcendental Awakening and Enlightenment. Following this, you can go on to consult with your peers in this regard, who have similarly learned the necessary skills and knowledge required to test this theory, and have then gone on to experientially test it. By consulting and comparing in this way, you can determine if *their* experiential results match your own, as a kind of peer review. The philosopher Ken Wilber has presented and carefully described this process of direct experiential testing of transcendental assertions and postulates in his writings.

VS: So Onliness theory is post-metaphysical in this important but limited sense.

Sage: That right. In this specific but important way, Onliness is, in a *primary sense,* a post-metaphysical theory and perspective.

VS: Also, you've talked about *uncontracted* Self-as-Self. What does that mean?

Sage: The controversial Sage Adi Da talks about ego's innately self contracted state of consciousness. He points out that within inherently self-centered narcissistic egoic consciousness, one reflexively and chronically tends to withdraw or *contract* from complete and open relationship to Supreme Reality. That is, one *chronically* and *habitually* pulls back, avoids and withdraws from authentic, profound and open relationship with other beings, dimensions and aspects of Reality. I believe Adi Da is correct in this understanding. Functioning in Self Awakened profound, spontaneous and open relationship to *all* Beings and Entities, without reservation or condition, is the natural and joyous Bliss of being in innate uncontracted relationship to *all* of Reality.

VS: What then does *unconditioned* Self or Spirit specifically mean?

Sage: It means that transcendent Self or Spirit is not relative or conditional, but rather is Absolute and Unconditional. Self-as-Self is not conditioned, determined or influenced by any circumstance *whatsoever*. For example, feeling wonderful does not bring one any closer to Self, nor does feeling miserable push one at all farther away from Self. Recall that Nondual Consciousness Realization Self is the Ground, Goal and Source of and from which all Consciousness arises, and to which It all returns; including the consciousness of any and all currently present conditional circumstances. And be Mindful that You and I are this Self of *Supreme Identity*, here and now, always and already.

VS: For me, when you say Self is Supreme, it implies that there is something else that is less than supreme.

Sage: There is nothing less or more than Self of Supreme Identity. Self *is* All and None; Everything and No thing. There is *only* Self, and Self *only*. To Awaken from the personal-egoic dream in which you're now so self involved, to truly Know Your Divine Self Identity, you must, moment to moment and day by day, facilitate this Awakening and Knowledge through your integral transcendental spiritual practice. To put it in Buddhist terms, you need to continue to turn the "wheel of the Dharma" or Truth; and in this Way also to turn back or reverse the "wheel of negative Karma".

VS: How can and do I go about actually *turning back* the wheel of negative Karma?

Sage: The negative Karma one creates, which involves the *turning away* from the transcendental Reality and Truth of Wisdom and Compassion, derives from feelings, thoughts, speech, actions and reactions of anger, hate, greed, possessiveness, delusion, ignorance, self importance, selfishness, self-centeredness, unforgivingness, impatience, vengefulness, jealousy, envy, duplicity, lying, deceit, deception, self contraction, indifference and so on. One can gradually eliminate or turn back the accumulation and compounding of such Karmic feelings, thoughts, speech, actions and reactions *specifically* in and through your meditation practice, but also, of course, in and through all of the other dimensions of your day by day and moment to moment integral transcendental spiritual practice. For example, one can turn back the wheel of negative Karma by and through the *Witnessing* of, focused attention upon, and progressive modification of such negative Karmic feelings, thoughts, speech, actions and reactions *as* they begin to arise and occur.

VS: Again, that's all easier said than done. Sometimes I just get very irritated and frustrated with people, and feel hateful toward and distrustful of them. I get sick and tired of their selfishness, indifference and stupidity. And indeed of *my own* selfishness, indifference and stupidity.

Sage: One can come to progressively *See* others, and one's own egoic self also, through the Eyes of Self or Spirit; that is to say through the Eyes of God-consciousness; in Loving Kindness and Compassion. Also, progressively dropping or dis-identifying from egoic self-importance and self-righteousness will help in this regard.

(Both sit quietly for awhile and then share a drink of water from their canteen)

VS: Why should I even *try* to change or lessen the stupidity, indifference and selfishness I so often see in this world? This is basically an endless, pointless, and futile task, don't you think?

Sage: As Self, this is not a distinct and separate task toward which You can seek. It's not a specific goal to which You can aspire, and toward which You can search. This World, and the stupidity, indifference and selfishness you as ego-self attribute to it, is *not* some dualistic *otherness,* separate and apart from You. As Divine Self, You *are* this very World completely, right here and now. And so, this World which You are, in all its integral unity and great diversity, and with all its many temporal problems, is *also* Divine. Certainly, to search and strive from the level of egoic consciousness to change this World can be beneficial, can reduce suffering, but *cannot* effect the radical transformative changes in human consciousness that humanity and this World so desperately need.

VS: How then, and in what way, can and do I function in this troubled world of birth and death?

Sage: Ordinary and everyday, just as You truly are. Function within Your integral transcendental spiritual practice as this *Suchness* Self of Everything and No thing that you already and always are. Just That.

VS: You make it sound easy and simple, but I have the suspicion that in fact it is not.

Sage: That's right. In Fact, Self Awakening to Spirit-as-Spirit requires extreme, disciplined and sustained practice, effort and struggle, which can effect a *radical* transformation of your ego-life existence. This in turn can open the gateless Gate of Nondual Self-as-Self Realization Consciousness. That is, Realization of Your Divine True Nature and Condition.

VS: Now that sounds easy enough, doesn't it? In other words, there's no simple and easy way through this ordeal of Self Recognition, Remembrance and Realization.

Sage: From ego-self perspective, that's correct. Very rarely are there earth-centered human exceptions that simply and readily overcome this difficult ordeal.

VS: Is there any hope, whatsoever, that I'm perhaps such a human exception to this requisite prolonged struggle of Consciousness transformation?

Sage: (smiles and gently laughs) No hope whatsoever. Nor, for that matter, is there any such hope for me. If it's of any comfort, we're members of a very large gathering of human beings in this category.

VS: So I need to continue my integral transcendental spiritual practice at interior-subjective and exterior-objective, individual and social-cultural-communal dimensions; the four quadrants. That is, the I, We, It, and Its quadrants in Ken Wilber's terms. And I must work on as many of my developmental-evolutionary realm-wave states and stages, as well as developmental lines, as possible.

Sage: That's right. But not just working *mentally* in your head. Also working beyond the mentality of ego consciousness ideas and conceptions, *trans-mentally* and *Heart-centered* in and as Supreme Reality. Developing in Divine Courage to transcendently Embrace and directly Acknowledge this Self Reality You are. And thus developing in Divine Wisdom, so as to Recognize and *openly* Confess that You are, in Fact, Reality Itself.

VS: Right now, that seems very far from me. I'm not at all at such a level of transcendent Consciousness Recognition, Acknowledgment and Confession. Meanwhile, I'm still somewhat confused as to what you're suggesting I do *here* and *now*, at my current realm-wave level and state of consciousness, to be helpful in relation to this world's suffering as it presently exists?

Sage: In the realm-wave of high vision-logic ego consciousness, within which you primarily function now, of course you must continuously and assertively employ and apply your own unique individual bodymind talents and abilities toward reducing the suffering of all beings, human and nonhuman, within the social-cultural, and indeed in all life realms. Likewise, you must continue to work toward reducing destructive factors in the physical-environmental realms that disrupt the ecological balance and sustainability of this living earth as a whole.

VS: Sage, your suggestions are supportive, and point me in the direction I'm already going and *want* to go in relation to others, and to the earth.

Sage: But understand that ego consciousness level works, efforts and applications by themselves cannot, and will not, effect a *radical transformation* of one's spiritual transcendental Consciousness, much less such spiritual transformations of Consciousness in others, that are so critically needed at this point in earth-centered human history. The transformational *focus* and *core* of such transpersonal, trans-egoic, trans-mental, and trans-rational Nondual Spirit-as-Spirit Consciousness Remembrance needs to *initially* occur interiorly and individually. However, the positive and constructive social-cultural and ecological-environmental results of such ego consciousness centered efforts, as an important dimension of your integral transcendental spiritual practice, can and do function to support a facilitative *context* within which such interior individual transcendental Consciousness transformation may occur.

VS: I understand what your saying. But the proportion of the human population that understands, *and* responds positively to, what you're saying is very small. Only a tiny portion of the world's human beings have the luxury, time, and energy available to them, and are at all interested in, carefully considering ideas of transcendent Consciousness and its transformation. Perhaps only five per cent of the world's population are even primarily functioning at a high vision-logic and worldcentric consciousness realm-wave level. And perhaps one percent of the human population have some degree of interest in concepts and ideas of transformation of transcendent Consciousness. The majority of this world's human beings work hard and long hours or have no or little employment at all, and often struggle to survive and minimally sustain themselves day to day on a subsistence or very low income level. In terms of consciousness levels and states of function, it's likely that a majority of the human population functions primarily at mythic realm-wave levels and states of consciousness, or below; not yet even reaching sustained and stable rational, much less vision-logic, realm-wave stages and states of consciousness. Indeed, you have a very tiny audience I suspect.

Sage: I think you're right. And currently, it's likely that only a tiny fraction of one per cent of earth-centered humans ongoingly function at transcendent transpersonal realm-wave levels and states of Consciousness. But still, this tiny fraction of human beings is very telling and important in terms of the human potential for transcendent Consciousness Remembrance and Realization. In this way, the potential of this same tiny fraction of one per cent is *so* important in relation to the overall human manifest expression of Beauty, Truth and Goodness in this world.

VS: Sage, I'm beginning to understand you, and what you say, much better now. I find myself more and more drawn to you as my spiritual teacher and guide. Drawn closer to your insights and understandings then I thought I ever would be. Is this foolishness and folly on my part, or development and growth?

Sage: That's something *only you* can know. A decision that only you can make. But Remember and be Mindful of *Who* You are, always have been and always will be; this unborn and undying Liberation and Freedom Self of Bliss, the Joy and Divinity of Worlds.

The scene slowing darkens and fades from view into blackness.

Act 2, Scene 3

Vagabond Scholar and Sage are sitting on a sandy beach in the shade of a palm tree, looking out upon the Pacific ocean breaking on the shore a few hundred feet away. The two share the beach with a few others who are round about them on this quite secluded southern California shore. They are located within and surrounded by a high-cliff rocky cove, with palm trees scattered here and there along the beach. The two figures partially face the audience, with a portion of the sandy beach, rocky cove and ocean also within the audience's view. It is a warm and sunny summer afternoon with a slight ocean breeze. There are the sounds of breakers tumbling at the shoreline and of sea gulls crying out around them. The scent of ocean smells are in the air. From time to time the two drink water from their shared canteen.

Sage: Innate-nature Self-as-Self neither comes nor goes, neither arises nor passes, but simply *Is*. This Supreme Self of no self is *Itself* God-consciousness, Christ-consciousness, Buddha-mind, Atman-Brahman. But understand that You and I *are* this Compassionate Omniscient Self of Radiance, and *only* That.

VS: You sometimes alarm me, even now, when you speak to me that way. When you express yourself like that I often have the fleeting urge to ask myself: Is this person some kind of "nut case"? Or at least ask: What in the *world* is this person talking about?

Sage: When I speak to You in this way, I'm addressing you *directly*, as You truly *are*. So, I'm speaking to Your true Nature and

Condition, as You deeply Know It to Be but refuse to, and will not, Confess It to Be.

VS: I understand. (pause) Sage, I've known you now for over seven years, and have continued my integral transcendental spiritual practice under your guidance and direction for nearly all that time. This practice has sometimes been frustrating and difficult, but overall its been a beneficial and fruitful time of transcendental spiritual development and growth for me. I thank you for your guidance and direction, and for offering and sharing with me your wisdom and compassion. I'm *deeply* grateful to you. But also, I remain somewhat, and sometimes very, *skeptical* of many of the things you say. And how you say what you say still greatly irritates me at times. I'm not sure whether these latter feelings and impression are a measure of my egoic ignorance, delusion and stubbornness, or rather a function of my grounding in sound judgment, practical common sense and sanity.

Sage: Probably both. But being cautious and skeptical is important in personal egoic life, and needs to be exercised and preserved.

(A brief period of silence falls between them.)

VS: In my meditation, ego consciousness sometimes seems to completely disappear.
It's then that a strange and foreign egoless Consciousness possesses my awareness and experience. A kind of calm and awake, yet empty Consciousness. It's as though I've temporarily lost my ego self. Sage, what are the changes in ego self that ultimately occur in transcendental spiritual development and transformation? What becomes of ego self and ego consciousness?

Sage: Ultimately You must die to exclusive ego self. Ego self and consciousness is thus included but transcended, negated and preserved. And You must come to Remembrance of *Who* You Truly are. Recognize that You are Radiant Spirit, *Self* of God-consciousness. Realize that You are this Self of no self that *is*

Godhead, *Only* and none other Than. Jesus speaks plainly and directly to this point: "The kingdom of God cometh not with observation. Neither shall they say, Lo here! or, lo there! for behold, the kingdom of God is within you."

VS: I don't know what to say.

Sage: Diligently, and as an *end* in and of itself, continue your open and inclusive four quadrant interior-subjective-intersubjective and exterior-objective-interobjective, individual and collective-communal, worldcentric to Kosmocentric transcendental spiritual integral practice. And do this *at* and *through* as many developmental lines and realm-wave states and stages as possible.

VS: I understand. But *what* and *who* is it you mean when you say "God-consciousness" or "Godhead"?

Sage: Transcendent Nondual Spirit-as-Spirit or Self-as-Self Realization *is* Godhead Consciousness, is Ultimate Reality. Whether We Awaken to It or not, each and every manifest Consciousness Entity of the Kosmos, including You and I, are always, already uncreatedly and boundlessly Realized as Divine Self of Nondual Consciousness; as God-consciousness Itself, as Absolute Reality without a second.

VS: What about the common and traditional conception of God that many, if not most, people associate with a this word?

Sage: That's not the conception of God I speak of here. This more common God conception emerges from a mythic realm-wave level and state of ego consciousness, and is seen as a *separate* transcendent Being, apart from humans, who creates, monitors and controls the destiny of all entities, human and otherwise. Such a God is a kind of "Great Father" or "Great Mother" figure who can love, care for and protect, and sometimes punish, his or her dependant and subject human beings. This God meets and satisfies the needs and requirements of earth-centered humans who primarily identify with the *mythic* realm-wave stage or level and state of ego-consciousness. This "Great Father" or "Great Mother" conception of God, co-constructed by humans within the developmental-evolutionary worldspace of their authentic mythic ego-consciousness realm-wave, is no more or less *real* than any other God or Godhead conception.

VS: But is not the God-consciousness and Godhead conception you describe more real and authentic, and thus more important, than the mythic-level consciousness God conception?

Sage: No. Both worldspace conceptions of God are equally authentic and real, and thus of equal importance in that sense, because both are formulated and derive from authentic realm-wave levels and states of Consciousness. However the God-consciousness or Godhead I describe from Onliness perspective emerges from the more Consciousness inclusive realm-wave levels of high vision-logic worldspace consciousness, and *above* this into levels of transcendent Consciousness, which are more advanced developmental-evolutionary realm-wave levels than is this more *metaphysically* oriented mythic realm-wave level of ego consciousness. In this way, from a developmental-evolutionary point of view, the Godhead and God-consciousness I speak of here has more intrinsic *depth* and *value* than the mythic level God conception, because it is more Consciousness inclusive. The Onliness Godhead and God-consciousness conception is a *different* conception of God from a different and higher, more Consciousness inclusive, worldspace realm-wave level and state of Consciousness, but it's not a more *real, authentic* or *important* conception of God.

VS: Does this degree of metaphysical orientation *difference* comparison then, between Onliness's high vision-logic and transpersonal Consciousness realm-wave level Godhead and God-consciousness conception *versus* the mythic consciousness realm-wave conception of God, have to do with your assertion that the Way of Onliness is, by comparison, a primarily post-metaphysical formulation?

Sage: Yes. One of the reasons Onliness theory is primarily post-metaphysical in nature is that it asserts, as others have also pointed out, that as human beings it is *We* ourselves who are finally responsible for the *direction* and *outcome* of our own human development and evolution. Thus, it is not the metaphysically designated mythic gods and their metaphysically postulated powers that determine human development and evolution. In this way, humorous self delusional assertions such as "the devil made me do it", although funny, do not hide or alter this human self-evolutionary responsibility.

VS: When you say *die* to the ego self, what does that exactly mean?

Sage: It is the death and dissolution of one's sense and certainty of being a *separate* self. This is the *radical* Recognition that the separate self you think yourself to be has, in Reality, no separateness at all. This ego death is the profound Awakening from the illusion of *otherness*; the transcendent deconstruction and death of egoic subject-object duality. But understand that this Awakened Realization of the death of ego self is trans-mental, trans-rational, and trans-egoic. In this developmental-evolutionary way, identity as ego self is *transcended* but included, negated *and* preserved.

VS: How is this ego-self death enacted and accomplished?

Sage: Your meditative practice plays an important role. Ultimately however, this involves *all* aspects and dimension of your integral transcendental spiritual practice; all four quadrants and all possible developmental lines, realm-wave states and stages. But understand that the death of ego self, of narcissistic self-centered ego consciousness, is most often a prolonged, and very difficult and painful ordeal.

VS: What then becomes of ego self and ego consciousness?

Sage: With the death of exclusive ego-self identity, the self of ego consciousness no longer solely pursues and serves narrow narcissistic and egocentric goals and actions, but rather is now enabled and employed to support, facilitate and serve transcendent Consciousness development and growth. In this way, such transpersonal Consciousness Awakening has transcended self of ego consciousness, but *also* has included it.

VS: Sage, I tend to dearly love my exclusive ego self and want it to live on. I don't want my ego self and consciousness to die, and would fight and struggle to keep it alive and functioning as it *is*.

Sage: My point exactly. Such death typically involves an effortful, protracted and ongoing struggle. And in this, exclusive ego consciousness subtly and endlessly plays devious, deceptive and duplicitous tricks and ploys within consciousness, trying to maintain its egoic ascendance and control. For example, ego consciousness might suggest that it's with you and on you your side in this struggle. It might secretively and quietly hide itself so as to be inconspicuous, and thus seem to disappear. It may step aside to stand next to you in order to objectify itself, then tell you how terrible it is. This goes on and on.

VS: But my ego self, my ongoing personal consciousness, *is* me. It's *who I am*. It's the only personhood I have.

Sage: At the exclusive identity realm-wave stage and state of ego consciousness, that's true. But in a more profound sense, at a deeper realm-wave level and state of transcendent Consciousness, You already Understand that this is *not* true. Beyond and including ego bodymind, You already Know, and have always Known, that You *are* Realized Nondual Consciousness Self of manifest Form and unmanifest Emptiness. This All-encompassing Alpha and Omega Self of Mystery.

VS: So I have different, and sometimes opposing, kinds of Knowledge at different realm-wave levels and states of Consciousness?

Sage: That's true. But *now*, as best you can, Become that which You deeply Understand Yourself to be. Move to Embrace that which You truly Are.

VS: I understand what you're asking me to do, but it's *beyond* me at this time. I now primarily identify myself with ego consciousness, as personal egoic self of bodymind.

Sage: And remember too, this ego self is very important. As a critical aspect of your integral transcendental spiritual practice, you need to *continuously* develop ego consciousness toward a more balanced and integrated, responsive, open, uncontracted, and mature ego self. That is, one that has liberated itself from the alienation and dissociation of personal psychosocial-emotional shadows, problems and disorders; toward a more authentic, truthful and integrated ego self and consciousness. And such ego-self integration and growth will *greatly* facilitate Emergence and Realization of transcendent Consciousness development.

(A brief silence falls between them.)

Sage: It's *so* simple. Nothing to be gained or lost. Selflessly just living, ordinary and everyday. Uncreated, prior to both time and space, neither coming nor going, unconditioned, boundless and omnipresent, this Self only, which Is *and* Is-not; yet is so *plain* and *clear* that It cannot and can never be something missed or found.

VS: So, there's this simplicity, obviousness and ordinariness to Enlightenment; to Self-as-Self Nondual Consciousness Realization. But to *me* life seems difficult, complex, challenging, competitive, often irritating and frustrating, unpredictable, obscure and confusing; and even dangerous, hostile and threatening at times.

Sage: I understand. This has been *my* experience also. And it's my impression that the *life of self* in ego consciousness is experienced by almost all humans pretty much in this same way. The death of exclusive consciousness identification as ego self puts an end to this kind of suffering, though not an end to the bodymind's afflictions and pain of manifest human embodiment itself.

VS: Sage, the teachings you share with me tend to focus heavily on interior-individual *subjective* consciousness, which is the *Beauty* or singular "I" quadrant, to put it in Wilberian quadrant terms. In so doing, you appear to de-emphasize our shared interior-collective-cultural *intersubjective* consciousness, which is the *Goodness* or plural "We" Wilberian quadrant.

Sage: This is true. Primarily, I wanted You to initially focus on the transcendent Ascent of Wisdom and Insight through development and growth of Your own individual-subjective *personal* and *transpersonal* Awareness and Experience. Since you've now noted this imbalance toward the individual-subjective Ascent of Wisdom, or Eros - which is the Creative Power of Love, it's time to begin to specifically emphasize issues of the immanent Descent of Compassion and Care, or Agape; this We, You and Thou which is equally important to, and indeed inseparable from, Wisdom, in the Awakening to Nondual Self-as-Self Consciousness Realization.

VS: In Wilberian terms then, work focusing on my interior-subjective *individual* consciousness - of Platonic Beauty, my interior-intersubjective *collective-cultural* shared consciousness - of Platonic Goodness, and my combined exterior-objective *individual* consciousness and exterior-interobjective *collective-social* shared consciousness - both of Platonic Truth, are all of *equal* importance in the day to day practical application of my integral transcendental spiritual practice. Is that right?

Sage: This is also true. These four integral and interactive, and thus basically inseparable, holonic-polaric quadrants of Reality that are invariably expressed in human development and evolution must each and all be, day to day, *equally* included into any authentic integral transcendental spiritual practice.

VS: I understand. Sage, exactly, what *is* Compassion? How do I recognize and express true and authentic Care and Compassion of and toward We, You and Thou in my daily life?

Sage: Compassion is the response of Care and Loving Kindness toward *all* Consciousness Beings and Entities. Compassionate response and action toward each and every such Being and Entity functions to reduce or eliminate pain and suffering, which pain and suffering manifests itself in a wide range of degrees and kinds. And *sometimes,* under certain circumstances, Compassionate response and action requires imposition, including self-imposition, of *firm* limitations, restrictions and prohibitions, accompanied by reasoned explanation and justification for such impositions, in relation to Beings and Entities, in order to lessen and eliminate suffering. Do not suppose that Compassion is always soft, yielding and tender.

VS: How should I approach the expression of Compassion in relation to other beings?

Sage: Openheartedly, with gratitude and humility, at having and taking every moment of opportunity to *serve* other beings, so as to lessen their suffering.

VS: Aside from earth-centered human beings, to what extent do you think other earth-centered beings experience suffering?

Sage: My impression is that *all* earth-centered, and indeed non-earth-centered, Consciousness Beings or Entities endure suffering; from grains of sand to a homo sapiens. And, in a relative sense, the more complex and consciousness inclusive the Entity, the more agony and suffering it tends to endure. I'm certain that there occurs widespread and intense agony and suffering in the full range of complex nonhuman earth-centered animal beings. And it seems clear to me that human actions in relation to such animal beings are responsible for much, if not most, of their suffering.

VS: What is the extent of earth-centered *human* suffering in your view?

Sage: For such complex and consciousness inclusive Beings, and at the current average developmental-evolutionary level and state of human consciousness we find ourselves, human agony and suffering in this world is *great* indeed. Right now, try to comprehend, accommodate and include *within* yourself the sum total of all of the diverse and unimaginable agony and suffering experienced and endured by each and every human in *this* moment throughout the world. Share each person's agony and suffering with *each* of them in this very moment; that is, accept and incorporate all of this suffering and agony *into* your own being and bodymind right now. This is at once heartbreaking, soul-wrenching, overwhelming and truly incomprehensible. In relation to earth-centered human beings, this is the profound and critical issue of Compassion and Care that must be *continuously* confronted and address in your integral transcendental spiritual practice.

VS: I understand and agree. But concerning earth-centered Consciousness Beings in general, how do I specifically go about the actual practice of Compassion in relation to the interior-intersubjective collective-cultural and the exterior-interobjective collective-social holonic-polaric quadrants; the two communal social and cultural quadrants of We, You and Thou?

Sage: Whenever and wherever you see the suffering of other Consciousness Beings and Entities, individually or as a group, employ and apply whatever skills and talents that are yours, and available to you, so as to reduce and eliminate such suffering. Bring as much time and energy as you possibly can in actively implementing your skills toward reducing that suffering, especially in the *human* social and cultural realms wherein you abide. And in these realms, apply your skills and talents at as many levels of human interaction and endeavor as possible. For example, apply them at levels of one-to-one individual, as well as at social, cultural, political, economic, aesthetic-artistic, scientific, literary, communicative, philosophic, entrepreneurial, and ecological-environmental levels of relationship and endeavor. In this regard, there's plenty of work to go around in this manifest world we inhabit.

VS: That's a tall and daunting order.

Sage: But it's the *commitment* of immanent Compassion that needs to be confronted and addressed, and that must be met, in transcendent Awakening to Nondual Self-as-Self Realization Consciousness. Remember, it is the Ascent of transcendent Wisdom and the Descent of immanent Compassion that are the two Luminous and All-pervading Directional Dimensions of Self-as-Self Consciousness Reality; which *Self* in Truth and Fact You are.

VS: I understand. But give me a *break*. I can't do all of this; I'm not capable of taking on this degree of compassionate responsibility.

Sage: In this, You only need to do the best you can, moment to moment, day by day.

VS: But even should I Realize Nondual Consciousness Enlightenment of Wisdom and Compassion, how would this *substantially* change this world for the better, toward greater goodness and compassion?

Sage: Awakening to Nondual Self-as-Self Consciousness Realization is neither a means or end, nor is it *not* a means or end. Vagabond Scholar, recall that to have a goal of *seeking* Enlightenment is the certain way to never Realize Enlightenment; a sure way to avoid Awakening to transcendent Self Reality. And to have a goal of seeking Enlightenment so that when Realized your goal is *then* to seek still further to change the world toward greater goodness and compassion, will certainly insure that the world will not and can not be changed toward greater goodness and compassion in this way. In Reality, You already are this World, and indeed You are the Kosmos Itself of *all* worlds and universes, without exception. You have no otherness; there is nothing that exists *beyond* or resides *outside* of You.

VS: What then is the purpose or reason for including in my integral transcendental spiritual practice the practical Compassionate day to day focus and work you've just described?

Sage: Your integral transcendental spiritual practice has no purpose. It is done for its own sake; it is an end *for* and *in* and *of* itself. Your practice does not *seek* Awakening and Enlightenment, but rather is *Itself* a direct Expression and Realization of Awakening and Enlightenment.

VS: I see. (pauses) Sage, again I find myself wondering, what is the point of it all? I see myself doubting this integral practice direction I've taken over these past years of my life.

Sage: The rational consciousness of ego-self does not want to be transcended and replaced from its preeminent position in Consciousness. It dreads and is fearful of Awakened Nondual Self-as-Self Consciousness transformation. And the reaction you describe is a natural expression of the protective function and survival predisposition of your exclusive ego self and consciousness. As I've said, there's *no point* of it all, *at* all. There's no goal to be sought or achieved. You always, already are Enlightened. So where now is the doubt? And why would you take any direction whatsoever *from* Enlightenment?

The scene slowly darkens and fades from view into blackness.

Act 3, Scene 1

Sage and Vagabond Scholar are sitting on a bench at the campus of Stanford University in California. They are seated along the south side of the Quad at Stanford with its long row of brown sandstone arches and its red-tiled roof of walkways and academic buildings in view behind them. It is a pleasantly warm and mostly sunny late afternoon with white clouds floating in blue skies. Students, staff and faculty pass by in the background and their voices can be heard. Birds fly round about and their quiet chirps and songs are in the air. The two share a bag of corn chips which each samples from time to time as they talk.

Sage: In meditation, *abide* as timeless, formless and unmanifest *Causal Emptiness*. Trans-pear as Radiant Truth of this Emptiness. Trans-ist as choiceless, actless, and boundless Freedom and Liberation Self that You already are, and always have been. Be Mindful that You *are* this very Causal Emptiness of unborn and undying God-conscious *Mind* of Mystery.

VS: Why do you emphasize the Consciousness of Causal Emptiness in my meditation?

Sage: First, understand that all of manifest Form ultimately derives from Consciousness. It is *from* Consciousness that all manifest physical matter arises, and *not*, as many claim, that consciousness is merely a byproduct or derivative of matter. It is *through* and *within* the open Ground of unmanifest, boundless and formless Causal Emptiness Consciousness that Awakening to the primordial Self is Realized. Primordial Self is this *pure Witness* of the Causal Reality of unmanifest, timeless and formless Radiant Holistent Emptiness (see Figures 3, 4 and 6).

VS: But how, in meditation, is my focused attention in Causal Emptiness of particular benefit to me?

Sage: Intently opening Attention to Choiceless and Actless unmanifest Causal Emptiness enables You to Confront and Recognize deeper trans-egoic, trans-mental, and trans-rational realm-waves of *transpersonal* Consciousness in meditation. From what you've said, it seems as though you often tend to drift toward egoic-mental constructs of consciousness in meditation.

VS: That's true. In meditation my mind often wanders into everyday life egoic-mental ideas, feelings, images and concerns. And at times, I do get discouraged and feel hopeless about the effectiveness and usefulness of this daily meditation practice.

Sage: Keep in mind that in serene reflection meditation you need to sit up straight and erect, without tension, with chin slightly tucked in, with the top and back of your head pointing toward the ceiling - *just* sit, *just* look. Let things arise - thoughts, ideas, feelings, sensations, images, visions - and let things pass; don't hold on and don't push away. To further facilitate this state of Mind you can focus attention solely on your natural breathing, on breath only.

VS: In meditation, how do I move *beyond* just passing Awareness of and *into* actual Realization of formless Causal Emptiness Consciousness?

Sage: Developmentally, through transformative transcendental Consciousness Awakening. This growing Awakening to expansive and open Causal Emptiness involves developmental transformation from Soul to Spirit Consciousness Recognition and Realization. This latter entails the *transpersonal* transformation from the Soul realm-wave of worldspace Subtle Prim-istence Consciousness, to the Spirit realm-wave of worldspace Causal Holistence Consciousness (see Figures 3, 4, 6 and 7). And this requires Focus and Attention not only in meditation, but also in *all* realm-wave stages, states and developmental lines of all *four* quadrants of Your integral transcendental spiritual practice.

VS: I see. But in my meditation practice, what specifically is involved in this transformation into the Spirit realm-wave of Causal Holistence Consciousness?

Sage: This is an advanced and profound, and at times shattering and difficult as well as joyous and blissful, transformation of transcendent Consciousness. It is *within* the developmental-evolutionary Consciousness realm-wave of Causal Holistence (see Figures 3, 4, 6 and 7) that there occurs the transcendent Realization of Your Identity as primordial Self of boundless and eternal Spirit. Here, the always already open Ground of *Holistent Emptiness* Awakens in Consciousness. Within Causal Holistent Consciousness of primordial Self is the *pure Witness* or Seer of the vast infinity of formless, boundless, and unmanifest transcendent Self Reality.

VS: Is this formless, boundless and unmanifest primordial Self of Consciousness the *same* as ultimate and supreme Nondual Self-as-Self Consciousness Realization?

Sage: No. This is the *primordial* Self of Causal Holistent *realm-wave* Consciousness. This *pure Witness Self* is unmanifest, formless and boundless, but is yet of realm-wave Reality; is of Causal Holistence realm-wave Consciousness that is to say. Nondual Self-as-Self Identity and Realization transcends but includes *all* realm-wave levels of Consciousness, but is *not* Itself transcended but included as a realm-wave. Thus, Absolute Self Reality Consciousness is not Itself a realm-wave *among* realm-waves, but rather is the "Realm-wave" of all realm-waves; is the Realm-wave Ground from which all realm-waves arise, and to which they all return. In this way, Nondual Self Enlightenment is *neither* a realm-wave *nor* is it not a realm-wave, and both. Recall also, that Nondual Self-as-Self is *neither* a holon-only or a holon-polar, *nor* not a holon-only or holon-polar, and both.

VS: I understand. But why do we need all of these realm-wave level and state gradations of transcendent Consciousness Awakening? What is the *use* and *purpose* of all this formal mental complexity?

Sage: You mustn't take these structured mental formulations too literally. They are simply various ways of attempting to describe, visualize and understand the developmental-evolutionary process and course of Awakening to Enlightenment. That is, they're *cognitive* efforts of insight to help one better comprehend the developmental-evolutionary Consciousness unfolding and growth of transcendent Self or Spirit. Again, in Buddhism such attempts and efforts contribute to, are a part of, the First Step on the "Noble Eight-Fold Path of Enlightenment" which is called "Right View". I would described this Step more completely as "Right cognitive-mental View."

VS: Sage, I have known and worked with you as my spiritual teacher and guide for nearly ten years now. I've learned much from you and have spiritually developed a great deal over these years. But I still feel I've made very *limited* progress and growth toward major transcendent transformational Consciousness Realization and Awakening. What is your impression?

Sage: In my view, your transcendent spiritual development and growth over this time has been *significant* and *substantial*. However, I do think you need to deepen and intensify your all-level and all-quadrant integral transcendental spiritual practice at this time. The pre-personal, personal and transpersonal transformations that you are making are challenging and difficult, to say the least. In this regard, remember to observe the Compassion of Loving Kindness toward and patience with Yourself, as well as toward and with other Beings.

VS: Sage, can you tell me how long, how much more of my life, will such a Transformation take; and how much more effort will be required on my part?

Sage: Awakening from the illusion of this exclusive personal-egoic consciousness dream you now live *as* and *within*, to Self-as-Self Realization of Nondual Consciousness Enlightenment most often requires many years of sustained work and effort, *if* such transformational Awakening and Realization occurs at all.

VS: That's not exactly a "pep talk" from my point of view, but I understand. How would you describe the Consciousness of One who is transcendentally Awakened? Exactly how would you define Nondual Spirit-as-Spirit Consciousness Enlightenment?

Sage: (In complete silence, Sage sits very still and without expression for one full minute, looking directly upon the face of Vagabond Scholar, who also looks upon Sage in somewhat puzzled silence.) Silence in the face of this question is the most adequate and truthful answer I can offer You. Vagabond Scholar, any description or definition of such Enlightenment from personal-egoic consciousness perspective, even from its high vision-logic consciousness, can *only* appear to be paradoxical and ultimately inherently self-contradictory. That said, I'll nonetheless, and somewhat foolishly, assert that the *central essence* of Enlightenment is Self, is Spirit; that which You always, already are. Thus, You are Consciousness of Enlightenment *Itself* and *Only*, without a second or opposite. Such Enlightenment is at once both a universal and singular *and* a highly diversified and individualized Awakening. As Awakening of Enlightenment, You have no apart-ness or otherness. And as Self, which *is* Enlightenment, You See and Comprehend and Are *all* perspectives, *all* at once. As Self of Enlightenment, You are Unqualifiable and Unknowable, yet easily Known and Unavoidably-Everyday Accessible. Birthless and deathless, Your are, as Nondual Realized Enlightenment, Self of God-consciousness Only and Alone.

VS: You don't mean just me, but rather that *each* and *every* Consciousness Being and Entity is Self of Nondual Awakened Enlightenment, is that right?

Sage: That's right. In Reality, each such Consciousness Expression is fully and equally Buddha-mind and Christ-consciousness in relation to any and all so called "Others", because there is *only* Buddha-mind and Christ-consciousness; there is *only* Self.

VS: But how can a quark subatomic particle be fully and equally Buddha-mind and Christ-consciousness in comparison to a human being?

Sage: As this Bliss of Absolute Reality Consciousness, as Divine Spirit, there exists no distinction or difference in this way between the manifest Forms of Consciousness Entities. Thus, both of these Consciousness Entities you mention are fully and equally Recognized and Realized as Buddha-mind and Christ-consciousness. However, in subject-object relative reality consciousness they are recognized and valued as *vastly* different and *unequal* in their respective Buddha-mind and Christ-consciousness capacities and Consciousness-inclusiveness. But even in relative reality, all manifest physical Entities, from quarks to humans and beyond, have and express *some* type and degree of Consciousness; remote, strange and foreign as such Consciousness may appear to personal-egoic human consciousness perception.

VS: Coming back to Emptiness Recognition in meditation, I *have* noticed that my consciousness transitions into various depths or states of Emptiness occur more rapidly and easily than was previously the case. It's quite remarkable, and surprises me at times. When I'm able to relax into or surrender to this unmanifest Emptiness, there occurs a great sense of openness, liberation, freedom, calm and peace. But this soon passes as my ego mind again asserts itself and begins to wander toward this or that pressing idea, sensation, emotional feeling, or concern. Is what I describe the thing you mean by unmanifest Emptiness Consciousness?

Sage: Yes, this is an authentic *temporary state* of unmanifest Emptiness Awareness and Experience, though not of Causal Emptiness Consciousness. Your meditative practice is deepening. At still deeper levels of meditation you'll tend to not even be aware of unmanifest Emptiness Consciousness until later, after this has occurred and passed. But *beyond* your interior-subjective meditation focus and within the broader spectrum of your overall integral transcendental spiritual practice, which includes Realities of Beauty, Truth and Goodness, how is your body, emotional-sexual, mind, Soul and Spirit integral work functionally developing in areas of self, culture and nature?

VS: Fairly well I think. I'm not a highly sociable or extroverted person, but I do actively promote and participate in a few progressive and humanitarian social, cultural, political and ecologic-environmental causes and organizations. In general, I tend to be an intellectually oriented person who *observes, analyzes* and *comments upon* more than I actively socially participate in, and attempt to shape the immediate flow of, everyday reality and existence.

Sage: This diversified integral work in Your practice sounds good. My only suggestion would be to further intensify your unique balance of body, emotional-sexual, mind, Soul and Spirit *participation* in self, social, political, cultural and ecological-environmental functional life activities. That is, to intensify what you're already doing.

VS: I'll carefully consider and make application of your suggestions in this way.

Sage: Onliness perspective encourages individual *self-direction, self-regulation* and *self-determination* in how to specifically define, pattern, implement and apply the broad outline and general elements of one's integral transcendental spiritual practice. Onliness recognizes that each and every Consciousness Entity, each human being for example, has a unique and original set of body, emotional-sexual, mind, Soul and Spirit predispositions, skills, talents and intelligences. And thus, in the case of human integral spiritual practice, each person is encouraged to *individually* determine, pursue and develop-evolve their own particular set of skills, talents and intelligences in a unique balance between body, emotional-sexual, mind, Soul and Spirit. That is, to do this self-directedly so as to develop *whatever* talents an individual may have in these domains, to *wherever* these talents may lead that individual within the broad contexts of self, culture and nature.

VS: I understand what you're saying. You've said that Nondual Self-as-Self Enlightenment is an Unmediated and Inexpressible Reality. What exactly do you mean when you say Unmediated?

Sage: Self-as-Self Enlightenment *is* Absolute Reality, *is* Truth, without a second or opposite; *is* Nondual Consciousness Realization Itself and Only. There is nothing underlying or behind It. It has no mediation or mediator, no implicit or explicit origination, cause, justification, or definable meaning. Self is the uncreated, boundless, timeless and ultimately ineffable "end of the line", and Its beginning too of course.

VS: Sage, how, if at all, can this *esoteric* individual Realization of transcendental Consciousness transformation, gradually occurring *one* person at a time, possibly relate to, or somehow *comprehensively* address, the practical and *pressing* immediate and serious challenges and problems of all human consciousness and existence; and indeed address the issue of human survival itself in this world here and now?

Sage: This is a deep and important question. One partial answer is that sometimes a single Realized Nondual Spirit-as-Spirit Consciousness human Being is able to greatly influence and motivate a large number of people with His or Her presence, actions and message. However, given that currently a great majority of earth-centered human beings function primarily at mythic, or at best transitional mythic-rational, realm-wave stages and states of consciousness, I see no *immediate* way to effectively and comprehensively address the problems implied, and also indicated, in the your question. I suspect that to authentically and comprehensively address the challenges that your question raises, there first needs to occur *individual* transcendental transformations of Consciousness in a large number of earth-centered human being.

VS: But is there enough *time* to do this before we destroy our own human earth-centered existence? What do you think, are we humans developing-evolving more rapidly toward the option of transcendent Nondual Consciousness Self Realization *or* toward self destruction and extinction?

Sage: Both, and quite rapidly. But *which* self-selected option We are most rapidly developing-evolving toward is, I think, an *open* question at this time. Earth-centered humans now have the potential and capacity to effect *either* developmental-evolutionary option. The overall, but meandering, telos or inherent evolutionary impulse of Consciousness, of Spirit, is toward transcendent Self-as-Self Nondual Awakening, Remembrance, and Realization. But that certainly does *not* mean that earth-centered humans as a species are pre-destined to such Awakening and Realization. If ultimately We human Beings, as temporally evolving and yet fully manifest Realizations of Divine Consciousness, do not evolve to such Self Awakening and Realization, I strongly suspect that other manifest Consciousness Beings already have and certainly will; on earth and/or in other worlds and universes of the Kosmos.

VS: As a human being, that doesn't reassure me all that much, or put my mind at ease. And knowing you, I suspect it wasn't meant to. So then, you're not too concerned whether in the course of evolution we earth-centered humans survive or not; or whether we as a community of beings evolve to Realize Self-as-Self Enlightenment Awakening, or not?

Sage: Seen through the Realization Eyes of Nondual Consciousness Self-as-Self there is no *otherness* or *separateness*; no species of manifest Reality somehow *separately* privileged and set apart. Spirit-as-Spirit does not "play favorites" because there are no *separate* favorites *set apart* to play. Personally, of course, I hope that We humans will survive and can further evolve in transcendental Awakening to and Remembrance of our True

Nature, as Divine Self. And I'm *somewhat* optimistic that we will.

VS: I understand. But how can I best facilitate and support such human survival through transpersonal Consciousness development-evolvement?

Sage: Vagabond Scholar, *Awaken* to Who You truly Are. That is the Way, the Truth, and the Light. And human survival will take care of itself.

The scene slowly darkens and fades from view into blackness.

Act 3, Scene 2

Sage and Vagabond Scholar sit in Zion Canyon National Park on a high plateau. They are seated in the shade of a small rocky cove near the edge of a vertical rock cliff that extends down several hundreds of feet below them. It is a bright and warm sunny afternoon. In front of and all around them are great towering red and white rock cliffs and peaks, set against a clear blue sky. Far below are still more rocky cliffs and peaks, but not as towering; and deeper still within the valley can be seen green juniper and other trees. Winding its way along the valley floor a fast flowing turbulent aqua-colored river is in view. Sitting alone, the two figures partially face the audience with all of this dramatic background scene of rocky cliffs, peaks and valley floor also in audience view. The scent of sage, sounds of gusting wind and songs of birds are in the air. From time to time as they talk each drinks water from their shared canteen.

Sage: It is in the Recognition and ultimately Becoming of, and Identity as, manifest Being's ever-evolving, contextual and pluralistic transcendent Fullness of *Form*, and unmanifest Nonbeing's ever-changeless, formless and boundless transcendent Freedom of *Emptiness,* that Self of Enlightenment finds Its *complete* Expression. And this is the Self You are, *as* You are right here and now.

VS: Then operationally, Self of Enlightenment Consciousness implies that one Recognize, Become and Identify as *all* manifest Forms that have evolved up to and including the present time.

And by all Forms, I assume you mean all manifest Consciousness Entities or Realities, including all of Their past and present developmental-evolutionary realm-waves stages, states and lines of Consciousness. Is that right?

Sage: That's right. But to be truly integral and inclusive, such Recognition and Comprehension cannot, and will not, be Realized through meditation or contemplation *alone*. As the philosopher Ken Wilber points out, meditation-contemplation deals only with an individual's interior-subjective awareness and experience; deals only with the upper-left of the four quadrants. The problem is, that such meditation-contemplation doesn't expose and reveal the profound *subconscious* contextual content influences of the other three quadrants that interact with and greatly determine this individual's interior-subjective ideas, feeling, thoughts, insights, vision, understandings - consciousness. And thus, no matter how *long* or how *deeply* a person meditates or contemplates, the strongly determining contextual content influences of the other three quadrants remain primarily *invisible* to that individual's interior-subjective consciousness.

VS: And so for each individual human beings, Enlightenment must come to include Conscious Recognition and Comprehension of the other three quadrant's profound individual-objective, and social-cultural-linguistic interobjective and intersubjective subconscious contextual content influence on that individual's interior-subjective quadrant's transcendent Insights and Understandings?

Sage: That's right. Full Realization of Nondual Self-as-Self Enlightenment must indeed *include* the Unveiling and Recognition that these hidden sub-conscious contextual content *influences* have upon individual interior-subjective Consciousness. These three quadrants then, individual exterior-objective behavioral quadrant, social-structural exterior-interobjective quadrant, and cultural-communal interior intersubjective quadrant, will require *extensive* examination and study so as to deeply Understand the interactive influences they have on individual interior-subjective quadrant Experience and Awareness. And again, as postmodernism has insightfully pointed out in relation to the pervasive influence of culture, because such subconscious social-cultural-linguistic contextual influences are mostly *invisible* to individual interior-subjective consciousness, they tend to *distort* and *betray* the Truthfulness and Validity of such individual interior-subjective transcendental Awareness and Experience interpretation.

VS: So, within my integral transcendental spiritual practice, I need to consciously observe and carefully examine and understand the influences, interactions, and implications of my involvement and participation in *each* of the four quadrants?

Sage: Yes. This is a central meaning of "integral" in integral practice. The perceptually interpreted co-constructed personal and transpersonal Experience, Awareness, Knowledge and Meaning that derive in relation to these four quadrant expressions of manifest Form Reality are *critically* important to the Truthfulness and Validity of Self Remembrance, Recognition and Awakening.

VS: Can you once again and further clarify for me as to why you quite often use the expressions "co-constructed" and "co-created"?

Sage: I use these, as well as the term "co-enacted", because, as postmodernism points out, and Ken Wilber insightfully applies in relation to the "myth of the given external reality", *all* human perception and realization is *interpretatively* co-constructed or co-created through the continuously arising and passing manifest worldspace realities of one's conscious and sub-conscious individual *interior subjective* and cultural-communal *inter-subjective* perceptual awareness and experience, including past and present influences, *interacting with* one's *interpretatively* co-constructed manifest worldspace realities of continuously arising and passing individual *exterior objective* and social-structural *inter-objective* perceptual awareness and experience, as both endlessly develop and evolve. From such co-

construction, moment to moment, there continuously arises whole *new*, *unique* and *original* perceptually interpreted worldspace realities of consciousness. However, even *this* human perceptual-interpretive co-constructed projected reality *process* and *perspective* is ultimately transcended but included, negated and preserved, with developmental-evolutionary emergence of the *all-perspectives-at-once* transcendent Awakening of Nondual Self-as-Self Consciousness Realization.

VS: I understand. Sage, in your view, what is the underlying meaning and explanation of, and overall rationale for, the existence and evolution of transcendent Nondual Self Reality and Consciousness?

Sage: The philosopher Ken Wilber, and others as well, have suggested that perhaps all of this derives from a kind of hide-and-seek playfulness that Spirit indulges in, so to speak. A kind of *play* in which the *One*, Spirit, *involutionally* casts forth Itself, Its Consciousness, *into* and *as* the Many; so as to develop and *evolve* once again back to the One. That is, to come to Remember and Realize Its own True Nature through such evolvement in this playful way; from Spirit to matter, to life, to mind, to Soul, and once again to Spirit.

VS: Is this your view also?

Sage: In my opinion, this is an *important* and at least partially correct explanatory hypothesis, but still one that is incomplete and oversimplified. It is certainly a possible and interesting explanation. But I suspect that, even within high vision-logic consciousness, current earth-centered human beings, myself included, lack the capacity to formulate a coherent, complete and rational answer to such a profound question. Overall, I disagree with the *endless cyclic* portion of this hypothesis, but agree with that portion of the hypothesis which describes Spirit's or Self's current involutionary and evolutionary casting forth of Itself from the One into the Many, then evolving back into the One.

VS: What is it about the endless cyclic portion of this hypothesis that you don't agree with?

Sage: I would suggest that in terms of meaning, motive, and reason for Supreme Reality, there is *neither* a rational metaphoric *nor* a literal explanation that can comprehensively encompass Nondual Self-as-Self Consciousness Reality. The involution-evolution *endlessly cyclic* casting-forth-of-Spirit descriptive explanation, on the face of it, necessarily implies the existence of time and space. The Self-as-Self Consciousness Reality that We *are* includes but *transcends* time and space; is prior to and not in any way a function of time and space. And thus, for me, this description as a deep and comprehensive ultimate explanation seems superficial; and especially so as an *ongoing* endless cyclic explanation. One *speculative* example of an alternative Supreme Consciousness Reality explanatory motive and description beyond this endless cyclic patterning, and also transcending space-time, physical mass and energy formulation inclusion as well, could be something like this: When the current Consciousness cycle of this and related universes, which are now structured by, and evolutionarily function within, expressions of space-time, mass and energy dimensions, is *completely* dissipated and exhausted in terms of these physical dimensions assumed by Spirit, there may, at the end of that last nanosecond of space-time, spontaneously occur an immediate transformational re-structuring and re-configuration of transcendent Consciousness, of Self or Spirit, into a kind of coherent and integrated Kosmic Consciousness Expression that *neither* includes space-time, and thus does not even involve development-evolution in space-time, *nor* the familiar atomic and chemically structured mass and energy dimensions we now know and understand. That is to say, from our perspective, a totally new and original and yet to us utterly inconceivable, unrecognizable and unspeakable, coherent and integrated re-configured Structure of transcendent Supreme Consciousness, of Self Reality, beyond, that is *without,* the Consciousness Reality of space-time, physical mass, and energy. But beyond *all* such speculation, I would assert that *Unqualifiable* Self or Spirit Is just That, and That only.

VS: You're *killing* me with all these words and thoughts. But nonetheless I thank you for *kind of* answering my questions. I think I know less now than I did before I asked these questions.

Sage: That's good to hear. This suggests you're Insight and Understanding is increasing.

VS: Sage, I have known and practiced with you as my guide and teacher for nearly thirteen years. This path of Onliness Awakening, with its own particular version of integral transcendental spiritual practice that you have taught, has helped me to spiritually grow and mature. I now transcendentally Recognize the nature of Reality, of Self, as my own True Nature and Condition. Know that I Am God-consciousness only and alone, and none other Than. Know that I Am uncreated and timeless All and None; this unfathomable ecstatic Mystery of Atman-Brahman Self-as-Self. This unbounded omnipresent Radiance of Am.

Sage: Vagabond Scholar, from my point of view in Onliness perspective, your individual interior-subjective realm-wave development appears to be ongoingly and stably near or at the culmination, and thus full Realization, of *Soul Awakening*. This is the gateless Gate to preliminary Recognition of *Spirit Awakening*. In this way, it is at the *transformational transition point* between Subtle Prim-istence and Causal Holistence, which in Onliness is the point of final integration of the realm-wave of *absolute* Subtle Holistent Prim-istence Consciousness (see Figures 2, 3, 4, 6 and 7). This is a very advanced realm-wave stage and state of individual interior-subjective transpersonal spiritual development and Realization.

VS: Again, I thank you for your teaching and guidance over these Awakening years on my journey of transcendent Self Recognition, Remembrance and Realization.

Sage: It's been my honor and privilege to be your guide and teacher on this Journey.

VS: Sage, I would like to come back again to more immediate and practical questions of earth-centered human survival, growth and development concerns. Issues that are worrisome and pressing from my point of view. For example, can you *specifically* describe for me what you think would constitute an optimal, if somewhat ideal, growth, facilitative and suportive social-cultural, economic and political environment for humans; for their transcendental spiritual development and transformation in *this* world?

Sage: Yes, but understand that I must describe such an ideal in terms of my personal ego-individual *mental-conceptual* ideas and opinions, which are strongly influenced and shaped by my own particular social, cultural and historical contextual conditions and environment. Thus, this is *not* at all transcendental *trans-mental* Insight and Knowledge. And before I share my thoughts for such an idealized earth-centered human environment, I must indicate my belief that *none* of these ideas can be successfully implemented and effectively function *unless* and *until* a vast majority, like 85 to 90 per cent at a minimum, of the world's adult human population has stably realized the *rational, individual-reflexive* and *conscientious* realm-wave consciousness level and state of human development. In relation to this level of consciousness development, such a majority of adult humans must have stably realized a *worldcentric* and *post-conventional moral* developmental level of care and concern for each and every person in this world. This is the minimally necessary human developmental foundation and basis that *must precede* implementation of the proposed social-cultural, economic and political changes I'm going to talk about.

VS: Since a large majority of the current human population appears to primarily function at moral *conventional* ethnocentric and mythic conformist developmental realm-wave levels and states of consciousness, and even to some extent below this at magic and archaic realm-wave levels, there exists a large gap between current humanity's developmental-evolutionary levels and the minimal realm-wave levels that you indicate need to be realized to implement your idealized earth-centered human environment.

Is this correct?

Sage: Correct. But given the current rapid rate at which world societies, cultures, economies, political structures and global technologies and communications are evolving, I believe that it is at least *possible* to realize this shift in human development-evolution in a relatively short historical period of time. And given this, an admittedly *formidable* and *monumental* given, my idealized social-cultural, economic and political world, one that I hope we're evolving toward, would be worldcentric, world-universal, inclusive, thoroughly democratic and egalitarian in character. That is, an all-peoples democratic *world community*, one-person-one-vote, representative government would be necessary. It would not at all be tribal, ethnic, sectarian, one-religion or nation-state in orientation. There of course should be smaller units of government under it, like world community local and regional government entities, but they would ultimately be responsible and accountable to, and under the full authority of, the democratically elected all-peoples world-wide community government.

VS: What do you see as the basic outline and fundamental character of such a *whole earth-centered* human community?

Sage: From my perspective, the structure and functioning of such a world community and government must be *foundationally* based upon the immanent *Descent of Self,* of Spirit, in Compassion, Communion, Loving Kindness and Care - the care of Agape from the One to the Many, *concurrently balanced with* the transcendent *Ascent of Self* in Wisdom, Insight, Meaning and Knowledge - the creative *Eros* from the Many to the One. These need to be the broad underlying, enduring and guiding *basic* transcendental Principles and Practices of such a world-centered community. And the central purpose and reason for discussion of such ideas and for such a world community itself, from *my* perspective, must be to facilitate and support One's transcendent Awakening and Realization of Divine Non-attaining All-ness Self; this *selfless* Self that every Being always, already truly Is. But clearly understand that none of these diverse and broadly defined Onliness perspectives I've described can be, nor are intended to be, *in any way* proposed, imposed or in some way required as a type of singular religious suggestion, viewpoint, dogma or mandate in relation to *any* earth-centered human being of such a world community. In this proposed world community and government, *each* individual person must decide upon and determine their own unique and particular spiritual predisposition and pathway; ranging from no spiritual pathway whatsoever to a great and diverse multitude of spiritual pathway possibilities and options.

VS: You need to be more specific about your world community proposal to help me understand. For example, what degree and kinds of authority and power would such a world community government have in your view?

Sage: Compared to the present, such a world community government would have the authority to, and indeed would, effect a *radical* worldwide redistribution of wealth or economic value, so as to maintain a very small and modest difference in wealth between those who are the most and those who are the least financially wealthy. Also, there needs to be, at any given point in developmental-evolutionary time, some just, equitable and specified degree of democratically determined and imposed social-cultural limitations on world population and growth, so as to balance human population numbers with ecological-environmental considerations of the earth's capacity to adequately support, accommodate and supply all of the needs for human life, and indeed for all life, at that point in time. Finally, there must be world community *requirements*, and a strong ethos, for an ecologically balanced and sustainable physical earth environment for all beings, now and for the long term future. That is, there must be strong regulation and oversight for environmental protection and conservation of the world's natural resources, including air, fresh water, oceans and soil, that all being depend upon for survival. All humans and their institutions must learn to diligently practice consuming only what is truly needed, and not wasting, polluting and over consuming. And also must carefully recycle material, and use *only* environmentally clean energy sources, which does not include nuclear fission based energy sources, which I think are inherently dangerous and toxic, so as to have an ecologically *balanced* and *sustainable* earth environment for all beings, now and for all future generations to come.

VS: More specifically, how would such a world government be structured and elected?

Sage: In this world community, the individual people of the world would *directly* and democratically elect *all* of their various representatives, from local to worldwide representatives. And all candidates for all offices would be afforded the same amount of government provided public money, in proportion to the level and degree of importance of that office, to spend for self presentation as a candidate. Candidates would not be allowed to either directly or indirectly add to this amount from their own money, or with money or favors from any other source. And *all* media outlets would be required by law to provide equal and adequate amounts of free time and space to all candidates for any given office. Thus, functioning democratically, *all* of the people of this world themselves, each one acting individually, must be the *ultimate* and *final* arbiters and authority in *all* basic social-structural, economic and political matters and decisions.

VS: What kind of economic structure and dynamic would you propose for such a worldcentric society and government?

Sage: Functionally, I think this needs to be predominantly a *bottom-up entrepreneurial*, creative, inventive-innovative, open and venturing worldwide economic structure and system. However, this economic system needs to be *carefully* and *continuously* overviewed and regulated by the world community government in relation to the ethics laws and practices established for it, at all regulatory levels, so as to insure that the economic system observes and maintains safety, fairness, honesty, and transparency in all aspects of its functioning. Especially in determining equitable pricing structures, all of the people, through their representative world-wide government, must play a *central* and ultimately *predominant* role in such price structuring. I think that the final broadly defined criterion each person should ask themselves ought to be: Is this economic endeavor, structure or activity in some way and to some extent, directly or indirectly, of real benefit, enjoyment and/or functional use to each and every human being on earth? If not, it is not something that should be developed or pursued. In this way, it is all of the world's people as a whole that must have the *final* authority and say in all basic and structural economic matters.

VS: What kind of rights, optional choices, and freedoms would you propose for individuals in your society?

Sage: First among such rights, I would say that the world-wide community government needs to establish *a* just, fair and equitable distribution of wealth and economic value among *all* people, so as to provide for and *insure* that each individual, as a constitutional unalterable right, has a sufficient, safe, and nourishing food and water supply, as well as environmentally safe and health-protected sanitation facilities. Also, as a right, such a government must *freely* provide each person safe, adequate, and comfortable housing and surrounding neighborhood recreation, open space and community facilities. A monetary voucher provided by the world community government could be distributed to each world citizen, as needed, to purchase such a modest home in such communities. Perhaps two people could combine their vouchers for a somewhat larger but still modest home. Again possibly using vouchers, I would also propose that such a world-wide government *freely* provide each individual options for and access to a high quality educational and vocational training system, extending from early childhood education to the most advanced and academically rigorous private and public university graduate school education. I would also propose that such a world-wide government freely provide an effective, efficient and complete research and treatment integrated health care system for use by each and every human being. Finally, this worldcentric democratic government must vigilantly and assertively recognize, guard and maintain each individual's dignity and security, their rights to life, justice, equality and liberty, their freedoms of expression, association, assembly, religious-spiritual affiliation and practice, mobility; among other rights.

VS:　What about financial and economic issues of income, costs, and work in your proposed utopia?

Sage:　(Sage smiles and gently laughs) I would propose that each individual have the right to regularly receive a world-wide government provided minimal adequate income over the full course of his or her lifetime, so as to provide for their various other non-voucher living expenses like transportation, utilities, clothing and everyday recreational activities. Also, such a worldcentric society-culture must be mandated and required to offer each individual, depending on each persons developmental level and natural interests, talents and capacities, the choice of productive social-cultural contributory *work* for which there would be a modest pay, but within a very narrow overall range of monetary payment across all types of work employment. Or, as an alternative, there could be a freely provided world community voucher for schooling-training to prepare one for such an employment option.

VS:　But what if a person decides that he or she does not want to, and is not going to, do any economically-oriented social-cultural contributory work or schooling, not now or ever in their lives?

Sage:　Most importantly in this regard, I propose that it would *always* be that individual's absolute right to accept and pursue, or *not* to accept and pursue, such offered work or educational options at any given point in that person's life. But I believe that all human beings have remarkable and unique inherent talents, skills and abilities, and that given the possibility and option, each will, of their own volition and accord, strive in various and often original and unexpected ways to employ and apply these talents, skills and abilities in the world. As Thoreau said "If a man does not keep pace with his companions, perhaps it is because he hears an different drummer. Let him step to the music which he hears, however measured or far away." And as Milton said, and I agree, "They also serve who only stand and wait."

VS: How is this world-wide community government going to find the money to *pay for* all of your proposed free options and income features?

Sage: I propose that, under its constitutional law, the world community government would be required to carefully monitor and maintain steep progressive taxation rates, without tax exemptions and loop-holes, uniformly across the board on all sources and types of income, even up to nearly one-hundred per cent at higher income levels. This would be a primary source of income for the free options and incomes I propose. It would also, as I mentioned, keep the gap between the lowest and highest income earners very narrow. In my proposal, no corporate legal structures or entities would be permitted, only companies. Thus another primary source of income for such free options and modest incomes within the all-peoples world community government would be steeply progressive taxes on monetary profits from such companies; which would also limit excessive profits, and in this way limit excessive size and growth of such companies. Also, not having the great costs of individual nation-state armies and expensive technological arms to pay for and support, but rather *one* world community police force, with only very limited, inexpensive and non-lethal, low-technology weapons, would make available significant financial resources to help cover the cost of these incomes, vouchers and options for each individual.

VS: If and when there are severe and possibly violent regional or individual disputes or conflicts in any area of community, about any issue whatsoever, how would police intervention occur to forcefully control and stop such conflict? And what if the individual or group involved had lethal weapons of any sort?

Sage: In this world community it would be illegal to plan, produce, possess or use any type or design of lethal weapon, be it atomic, biologic, toxic chemical, laser, explosive, projectile or otherwise.

This lawful prohibition would be *strictly* and *carefully* monitored, over-sighted and enforced *world-wide,* at all levels of world community government. Police would promptly locate and arrest, or physically disable, anyone or group who plans, produces, possesses or attempts to use such lethal weapons. The legal consequences and punishment-incarceration for such a violation would always be very severe, if those involved are found guilty in a court of law. Simply put, there would be *no* planning, production, possession, use or existence of any type of lethal weapon, whatsoever, permitted in the world community I propose. To prevent ethnic-sectarian group-think "them-versus-us" mentality, I would suggest that such a world community police force be comprised of individuals so as to equally represent all regions and areas of the world, and represent all regions in this way at all levels of such an organization. And that such a worldcentric police force be allotted the minimally necessary but sufficient power and combative resources, excluding lethal devices or weapons, to quickly control and forcefully disable, if need be, those involved, so as to stop such conflict on all sides of the dispute, but *without* killing or seriously injuring anyone. However, the ultimate leadership and *final* authority and command of such a police force, the "commander-in-chief", must be the democratically elected highest world community leader, or leaders, and such a person, or people, must be world citizens and not in any way affiliated with or a member of the world community police organization itself. Such a police force must always be *completely* under elected civilian command and control.

VS: Your proposals sound very "pie in the sky" to me. I'm glad you don't expect too much of human beings in this world.

Sage: (Sage smiles) None of these proposals are new, strange, and certainly not original. I suspect that every thoughtful person, in one way or another, has thought about and understands that *some* version of these kinds of societal-cultural, economic and political proposals, as well as several others, will have to ultimately, and perhaps soon, be confronted, addressed, and accomplished in order to enable human survival and growth.

And this, in turn, can perhaps enable us to Realize our developmental-evolutionary human potentials.

VS: Although very general and sketchy, your idealized social-cultural, economic, political and earth-environmental proposals for human survival and growth are interesting and carefully reasoned. But also very *unrealistic*, given today's earth-centered human proclivities, conditions and circumstances. However, I thank you for sharing them with me.

Sage: In general, I agree with what you've said about my proposals. But I think the time we humans have left to accomplish the kinds of preliminary realm-wave developmental-evolutionary shifts in human consciousness I discussed, as well as to *substantially* address the individual, environmental, social-cultural, economic and political problems that we face, appears to be quite short in historical terms. We need to begin to take *bold transformative action* to address these issues here and now. The *open* question is, do we humans have the courage, will, and resolve to take such action here and now?

The scene slowly darkens and fades from view into blackness.

Act 3, Scene 3

Sage and Vagabond Scholar are seated together on a high cliff on a tropical island in Hawaii. The two sit overlooking a gigantic and verdant deep ravine that opens far below to distant rocky coves and sandy beaches, and beyond these can be seen the vast and blue Pacific Ocean. They sit in seclusion on the grass at the top of this ravine, at the very edge of a steep and towering cliff. It is a warm and breezy late morning and the sun is glistening on the ocean waters. The audience views these two face-on from an angle so as to see them looking out upon the ocean, but also the audience sees a portion of the ravine, rocky coves and ocean view beyond them far below. Brightly colored tropical flowers bloom around them here and there, and the quiet songs of birds are in the air. They share a water canteen from which, as they talk, each drinks from time to time.

Sage: Your True Nature and Condition is *All* and *Every*, *Each* and *Only*. As Universal Nondual Self-as-Self Enlightenment, this All-pervading Light and Luminosity of Worlds, your clinging exclusive identification *to* and *as* self of egoic bodymind must finally surrender to this True Nature and Condition that You are; must completely transcend ego-self, but include it also. This *letting go* of narcissistic exclusive ego self and its self-contractions is very difficult. But such *release* and utter abandonment, though painful, must occur. Finally, there can be no holding back, no reservation or evasion, from the unfolding of *direct* and *immediate* Recognition of Spirit-as-Spirit

Consciousness. Fearlessly, there is no turning back or hiding from this *plain* and *obvious* Radiant Awakening to Who and What you Are. Let go then of all ignorance and delusion, and *See complete* the All and Every, Each and Only Divine Self of manifest Form and unmanifest Emptiness You Are. Beloved, Awaken and dream *no more*.

(A brief period of silence falls between them)

Sage: Beyond your bodymind self, who are You?

VS: Including bodymind self, I Am that I Am; the very *Consciousness* of God. About this, I am *certain* in my mind, but not as certain in my Heart.

Sage: You once told me that our ego bodymind self is all there is. That there *was* no life or personhood, no self, beyond *this* self and consciousness, and that it was pretense to think it so.

VS: It was in ignorance when then I spoke to you. I now *Know* and *Confess* to You Who I Am. Birthless and deathless, I Am the Awakened One of Self-as-Self Absolute Reality.

Sage: Do You say this now because you think that's what I *want* you to say?

VS: No. This is truly How and What I Am. With humility, without self importance or merit attribution, individually-interiorly I Am resolved and steadfast in *Recognition* of this Self that I always already Am, and ever will be. There is now for me a letting go, an opening and surrendering of exclusive ego self to this Awakened Self of Bliss and Freedom. This Nondual Consciousness of Divine and Radiant Supreme Identity. This Spirit-as-Spirit Luminous Self of Mystery. No longer is there any reservation, hesitation or turning back from this boundless, timeless, uncreated Self I Am.

Sage: But *exteriorly* and socially-culturally-communally can You *be* this Self You are unto and of the World? Can You now bring this Self You truly Are *in* and *as* the World, and indeed Kosmocentrically *in* and *as* all Worlds? Vagabond Scholar, are You able to *Realize* Who and What You are *within*, and *of*, and *as* the World?

VS: I'm hopeful that I can and will, but still have reservations in this way. I have fears and doubts in this regard. Living as best I can through Compassion, Loving Kindness, Truth and Wisdom, moment to moment and day by day, within, of, and as this World is *very* difficult.

Sage: Yes it is. But trust Your True Nature and Condition; this Non-attaining *All-ness* Self of Mind. Apply the Buddha's Middle Way, with which the Way of Onliness accords; the Way of equanimity, balance, moderation, restraint, steadfastness, flexibility and reserve in this Endeavor, and indeed in *all* endeavors. Of the Tao, a Way in harmony with the Watercourse-way.

VS: But can I succeed not only in *Recognition* but also in *Realization* of Nondual Spirit-as-Spirit Consciousness *in* and *as* the World?

Sage: This success you speak of implies that action is done and attains the fruit of something called "success". Keep in Mind the words of the *Bhagavad-Gita* in this regard: "Do not say: 'God gave us this delusion.' You dream you are the doer, you dream that action is done, You dream that action bares fruit. It is you ignorance, it is the world's delusions That gives you these dreams." Also keep in Mind that ideas of success imply issues of discrimination, judgment and comparison, which is a *false* way. Live moment to moment directly, truthfully, fearlessly, and straightforwardly, right here and now. Bloom in Wisdom and Compassion plain and openly, exactly *as* and *how* You are; which is this Flower of All and None, of Every, Each and Only. This is Enlightenment. This is Self-as-Self *Absolute Reality*.

VS: Sage, how then can I Know when I've reached such a turning point of Spirit; this critical axis of Nondual Self *Realization* Consciousness?

Sage: Deep within Self, You will immediately Know that in this very moment just such a Spiritual turning point has always, already Occurred. When This is so, it may be that You are with Someone and looking intently into the eyes of this Person, who is in profound and utter suffering, despair, disorientation, bewilderment, confusion and fear, and this Person immediately Sees and Understands that You *Are* and *Know* Him or Her *fully* and *completely*, here and now. And You too *directly* Understand that You completely *Are* and *Know*, and in this way *Share,* the burden of such pain and suffering, and thus lessen this Person's pain and suffering. This is *one* way to See and Know the Realization turning point of Spirit, of Self, that You speak of.

VS: I understand. And yet, for me, this fortified and towering wall, this seemingly impenetrable barrier, of ego-self and ego consciousness seems to block and obstruct such Realization at each and every turn in life.

Sage: Mindfully Observe and Witness how you function in designing, constructing and executing ego self moment to moment in everyday life. *See* your own ego self and consciousness occurring, *as* it occurs. Notice, moment by moment, how you respond, act and react as ego self in relation to other people. Observe the specific functioning examples of self importance, self-contraction, selfishness and self-centeredness in egoic self and life *as these occur.*

VS: That should keep me *very* busy. Will doing this change my tight grip upon and fixed identification *with* and *as* exclusive ego self? Will it tend to break through this formidable egoic wall and barrier?

Sage: Yes. Such Mindfulness will tend to reveal in highlight so as to objectify exclusive ego life and consciousness; that is, make of it an object to be *Observed,* but now from perspective of a higher and more Consciousness inclusive transpersonal realm-wave level and state of developmental Awakening. In this way, ego self and consciousness become an *object,* as opposed to *subject,* from which You may now *dis-identify*, and thus, in development and evolution, transcend but include.

VS: Sage, I have known you as my guide and teacher now for fifteen years. Yet, for me, you still seem a rather strange and puzzling person. And somewhat intimidating at times, from my perspective. Of course I have great respect and affection for you, and am profoundly grateful to you for the guidance and teaching you have offered me over all these years. And I thank you for that.

Sage: You're most welcome. Beloved, I too have great respect and affection for you, and am grateful to you for permitting me to be your guide and teacher over these many years. Certainly, we both still have much work to do in our respective Journeys of the Spirit. But also, we've both come a long way on our shared Nondual Self-as-Self Recognition and Realization journey of Consciousness Awakening. At the same time, Understanding that, in Reality, there's been no journeying that has occurred at all, as We are of course always, already fully and completely the transcendent Self of which We speak. There is thus in Truth no coming or going in this regard.

VS: Sage, specifically how can I Recognize that there is occurring differentiation of and dis-identification from ego self in transcendent transformational spiritual development?

Sage: Understand that without Awakening to the immanent Descent of Compassion and Care, there can be no Wisdom. And without Awakening to the transcendent Ascent of Wisdom and Truth, Compassion cannot emerge and manifest. Thus, in complete Forgiveness to all Beings, including Forgiving yourself, Your *every* thought and action, great or small, must centered on *Concern for* and *Care of* each and every Consciousness Being and Entity, so as to lessen and eliminate each One's suffering. When You Recognize such Forgiveness and Compassion in every thought and action that You take, *then* You will immediately Recognize the *measure* of exclusive ego self dis-identification, the measure of Your ego self transcendence but inclusion. And in this, You will Recognize the *proximity* of your self-absorbed, self-contracted, self-important and self-centered exclusive-identity ego death.

VS: I understand, but that sounds very difficult.

Sage: The selflessness of Self is not so difficult. Such Forgiveness and Compassion occur gradually in the course of Consciousness *transformation* that derives from Your integral transcendental spiritual practice in the world. In this way, selfless Self emerges as You more inclusively *See* Beings and Entities through the Compassionate Eyes of Awakened Nondual Self; that is, through the Eyes of God-consciousness.

VS: Sage, I *too* wish to become a transcendental spiritual teacher and guide in and as a part of this everyday rough and tumble world. How should I approach and prepare for this transformational way of teaching? What do I need to do?

Sage: Continue, and even intensify, your integral transcendental spiritual practice. Study about such spiritual teachers, and also, if possible, talk with others that you know and trust who are knowledgeable and developed in the practice of such transcendentally centered spiritual teaching and guidance.

VS: Do you think I'm now ready to actively become such a spiritual teacher and guide?

Sage: Ultimately, this is a decision that You *alone* must make. However, I believe that You're ready to *prepare* to become a transcendental spiritual teacher and guide, but *not yet* ready and fully prepared to actively *be* such a teacher and guide. For now, continue in the ways and direction I've just indicated. I'll meet with you one year from now in Los Angeles, and again address this question you have for me. In the meantime, continue your integral transcendental spiritual practice with particular emphasis on ego self and ego consciousness awareness, development, and integration; with involvement in ongoing and in-depth counseling or psychotherapy if and as needed. A mature and integrated *personal* egoic self is the foundation for continued *transpersonal* ego self transcendence but inclusion. A person of *integrated* and *mature* ego self can unconditionally love, nurture, openly and emotionally respond to, protect, and be fully responsible for those Beings who are in close relationship with, and who depend upon, him or her in life.

VS: I understand.

The scene slowly darkens and fades from view into blackness.

Act 3, Scene 4

Vagabond Scholar and Sage are seated together on the grassy mall adjacent to Royce Hall at the University of California, Los Angeles campus in Westwood. Each has a sack lunch from which they eat sandwiches, a piece of fruit and peanuts, and drink water from their shared canteen as they talk. Students, faculty and staff are seated on the grass about them and stroll by them on this warm and sunny early afternoon. Bright red flowers bloom on the bushes next to Royce Hall. Scattered white clouds float high above. The songs of birds and quiet voices of passing people fill the air. They are seated mostly facing the old UCLA Main Library across from Royce Hall. The audience sees them face-on so that both they, the grassy mall and the front of Royce Hall are in the audience's view.

Sage: In relation to your life of ego self and ego consciousness development and maturation, are you now able to unconditionally love, nurture, openly and emotionally respond to, protect, and be fully responsible for those Beings in close relationship to you, and who depend upon you?

VS: Yes, predominantly I am. But in my focus on ego integration and maturation, which occurs within the context of my transcendental integral spiritual practice, I've found it necessary to involve myself, both in the past and presently, in ego consciousness level psychotherapy, and plan to continue in this therapy for now.

Sage: Good. But remember also, the death of exclusive ego self identity must occur if there is to be Self Remembrance and Realization. (Sage pauses for a moment) Understand, as the philosopher Ken Wilber points out, that the meaning of Causal Holistent Emptiness Consciousness is that It's not a *state* of Consciousness among other states, but rather is Itself the *Condition* of all states of Consciousness. Such Causal Emptiness is Self Remembrance, is Undivided Mind Awakening. And *You* are this Emptiness Itself and Only, without an opposite or second.

VS: This makes me sound rather self-important.

Sage: Only if you're *centrally* identified with ego consciousness, and abide in your attachment to identity as ego self alone. Choicelessly, in Actlessness, Self neither comes nor goes, neither abides nor does it not abide, and both. You are the very evolving *Self* of God, and *Realize* It not. Have You come to at least fully *Recognize* this Ultimate Reality You are?

VS: I *have* and *do*, at least in Recognition.

Sage: There is and can be no egoic pride or self importance, no merit, exceptionality or specialness in This at all. This is because Self-as-Self Awakened Consciousness has no otherness, exclusion, specialness or separateness *whatsoever* about or of It. It's this winging bird right *there* (Sage points) that now sings to us; It's completely ordinary and everyday. It's Nothing at all, and Everything. In Truth, Self is *Unspeakable*.

VS: I understand. I'm more and more Aware of letting go of ego selfishness and self-importance. And I Know that this Nondual Consciousness I Am is not an Experience or an Awareness, but rather is the Unknowable Source, Ground and Goal of *all* Experience and Awareness. And I now Realize that with the transcendence but inclusion, and thus *dissolution,* of dualistic subject-object consciousness, this *Nondual* Consciousness Remembrance and Awakening that I Am is at once both Seer and the Seen.

Sage: I understand. But specifically, *Who* and *What* is It You assert Yourself to be?

VS: Sage, I Am Self of Nondual Spirit-as-Spirit Consciousness; timeless, boundless, unmediated, unconditioned and unconditional. I Am Nondual Realization's Radiant Omnipresent Self, Openly and Freely arising and emerging, Ascending and Descending, *as* the World; indeed, as the Kosmos of All Worlds. As ego self, in loving kindness, humility and gratitude, I have *no* fears or aspirations now. I Am Christ-consciousness, Buddha-nature, Atman-Brahman. This unfathomable *Self* of Wisdom and Compassion *in* and *of* and *as* the Kosmos; eternally and only. All-embracing, I Am All and None, Each and Every; Alpha and Omega. I Am the very *Consciousness* of God. But certainly I don't assert that *any* of This is True at the realm-wave level and state of exclusive identification *with* and *as* bodymind self of ego consciousness.

Sage: All that you have said is True. But *also*, as manifest and very fallible bodymind ego consciousness Beings, still, as Voltaire's Candide said, "we must cultivate our garden".

VS: I understand. (VS pauses) Sage, do you think that I'm now prepared and capable of effectively teaching and guiding others on their transformational transcendental spiritual journey?

Sage: As I've told you, this is a decision that *only* you can make. But I believe that you are indeed now prepared and capable of being such a teacher and guide to others. If someone seeks you out and asks that you be their transcendental spiritual teacher and guide, I think you are fully prepared to do so, and I hope that you do.

VS: Sage, is this the *last* time that you and I will personally meet with one another in this lifetime?

Sage: Yes. (Sage pauses) I've now taught you what transcendental spiritual Knowledge and Understanding I have to offer, as best I can. I've taught you all I can impart to you *at* and *through* this realm-wave level and state of high vision-logic consciousness. And it's my observation that over these sixteen years of our relationship you've greatly grown and developed spiritually, so as to Realize a *profound* transpersonal transcendental Consciousness Awakening to Nondual Self-as-Self, via the Onliness Way or Journey of Enlightenment. But I still want you to continue the full range and intensity of your integral transcendental spiritual practice, with continuing emphasis on its meditation practice. And be Mindful that the Reality of Spirit's transcendental manifest Form still and ever *continues* to evolve.

VS: I understand. Beloved, I am *so* grateful and thankful to you for being my transcendental spiritual teacher over these many years. And I will greatly miss you and our times together.

Sage: I *too* am grateful and thankful to you for being such an insightful, strong and persistent, if sometimes stubborn, student over these years of our relationship. And I too will greatly miss you and our times together. But you no longer need me personally to be your teacher and guide.

VS: But if there comes a time when I *do* need you once again to teach and guide me, what will and can I do?

Sage: Beloved, there is no *otherness* that separates You and I. *I Am* Your very Self, and *You* Are the very Self I Am. Recall what I once told You long ago: Here I Am. The Way I teach is the Way of Onliness Awakening to Enlightenment. If you want to learn, I Am *with* You as Your teacher at *any time* and *always*.

VS: I understand.

The scene slowly darkens and fades from view into blackness.

References

Adi Da Samraj (Da Free John) (1985). *The Dawn Horse Testament of Heart-Master Da Free John*. Middletown, CA: The Dawn Horse Press.

Adi Da Samraj (1995). *The Knee of Listening: The Early-Life Ordeal and the Radical Spiritual Realization of the Divine World-Teacher*. Middletown, CA: The Dawn Horse Press.

Aurobindo. (1990). *The Future Evolution of Man: The Divine Life upon Earth (3rd ed.)*. Pondicherry, India: Sri Aurobindo Ashram Press.

Blofeld, J. (translator and editor) (1968). *I Ching: The Book of Change*. New York: E. P. Dutton and Co.

Cohen, A. (2002). *Living Enlightenment: A Call for Evolution Beyond Ego*. Lenox, MA: Moksha Press.

Huxley, A. (1944). *The Perennial Philosophy*. New York: Harper & Row.

King James Version. *The Holy Bible*. New York: World Publishing Co.

Lama Surya Das (1997). *Awakening the Buddha Within*. New York: Broadway Books-Bantam Doubleday Dell Publishing Group, Inc.

Legge, J. (translator and editor) (1964). *I Ching: Book of Changes*. New York: Bantam Books, Inc.

Mitchell, S. (compiler) (1991). *The Enlightened Mind: An Anthology of Sacred Prose*. New York: Harper.

Reps, P. (compiler) (1989). *Zen Flesh, Zen Bones: A Collection of Zen and pre-Zen Writings*. New York: Anchor Book-Doubleday.

Suzuki. D. T. (compiler) (1960). *Manual of Zen Buddhism*. New York: Grove Press, Inc.

Swami Prabhavananda and F. Manchester (translators and editors)

(1957). *The Upanishads: Breath of the Eternal.* New York: The New American Library-Mentor Books.

Swami Prabhavananda and C. Isherwood (1960). *The Song of God: Bhagavad-Gita.* New York: The New American Library-Mentor Books.

Treon, M. (1981a). "Organismic communicology: a prologue - dead leaves and living shadows moving in the wind". *Papers In Linguistics: International Journal of Human Communication,* 14 (1), 131-148.

Treon, M. (1981b). "Organismic communicology: a second prologue - reflection, shadow and illusion". *Papers In Linguistics: International Journal of Human Communication, 14 (3), 359-375.*

Treon, M. (1989). *The Tao of Onliness: An I Ching Cosmology - The Awakening Years.* Santa Barbara, CA: Fithian Press.

Treon, M. (1996). *Fires of Consciousness: The Tao of Onliness I Ching.* Goodyear, AZ: Auroral Skies Press.

Treon, M. (2009). *Uncreated Timeless Self of Radiant Emptiness - Onliness Consciousness and Commentaries: Formulations of a Post-metaphysical Integral Transpersonal Communicology.* Goodyear, AZ: Auroral Skies Press.

Whitehead, A. (1967). *Science and the Modern World.* New York: Macmillan.

Wilber, K. (1980). *The Atman Project: A Transpersonal View of Human Development.* Wheaton, IL: Quest.

Wilber, K. (1981). *Up From Eden: A Transpersonal View of Human Evolution.* New York: Doubleday-Anchor.

Wilber, K. (1983). *Eye to Eye: The Quest for the New Paradigm.* Boston: Shambhala Publications.

Wilber, K. (1984). *A Sociable God: Toward a New Understanding of Religion.* Boston: Shambhala Publications.

Wilber, K. (1995). *Sex, Ecology, Spirituality: The Spirit of Evolution.* Boston: Shambhala Publications.

Wilber, K. (1996). *A Brief History of Everything.* Boston: Shambhala Publications.

Wilber, K. (1997). *The Eye of Spirit: An Integral Vision for a World Gone Slightly Mad.* Boston: Shambhala Publications.

Wilber, K. (1998). *The Marriage of Sense and Soul: Integrating Science and Religion.* New York: Random House, Inc.

Wilber, K. (2000). *One Taste: The Journals of Ken Wilber.* Boston: Shambhala Publications.

Wilber, K. (1999-2000). *The Collected Works of Ken Wilber,* Vol. 1-8. Boston: Shambhala Publications.

Wilber, K. (1999-2000, vol. 4). *Integral Psychology: Consciousness, Spirit, Psychology, Therapy.* (in *The Collected Works of Ken Wilber,* vol. 4). Boston: Shambhala Publications.

Wilber, K. (2004). *The Simple Feeling of Being: Embracing Your True Nature.* Boston: Shambhala Publications.

Wilber, K. (2007). *Integral Spirituality: A Startling New Role for Religion in the Modern and Postmodern World.* Boston: Integral Books-Shambhala Publications.

Wilber, K., J. Engler and D. P. Brown (1986). *Transformations of Consciousness: Conventional and Contemplative Perspectives on Development.* Boston: Shambhala Publications.

Wilber, K., T. Patten, A. Leonard and M. Morelli (2008). *Integral Life Practice: A 21st Century Blueprint for Physical Health, Emotional Balance, Mental Clarity and Spiritual Awakening.* Boston: Integral Books-Shambhala Publication.

www.ingramcontent.com/pod-product-compliance
Lightning Source LLC
Chambersburg PA
CBHW061740020426
42331CB00006B/1301